TEA

Designed by Eddie Goldfine
Layout by Ariane Rybski
Edited by Shoshana Brickman
Photography by Danya Weiner

Library of Congress Cataloging-in-Publication Data Available

10 9 8 7 6 5 4 3 2 1

Published by Sterling Publishing Co., Inc.
387 Park Avenue South, New York, NY 10016
© 2009 by Penn Publishing Ltd.
Distributed in Canada by Sterling Publishing
$^{c}/o$ Canadian Manda Group, 165 Dufferin Street,
Toronto, Ontario, Canada M6K 3H6
Distributed in the United Kingdom by GMC Distribution Services,
Castle Place, 166 High Street, Lewes, East Sussex, England BN7 1XU
Distributed in Australia by Capricorn Link (Australia) Pty. Ltd.
P.O. Box 704, Windsor, NSW 2756, Australia

Sterling ISBN 978-1-4027-5232-2

For information about custom editions, special sales, premium and
corporate purchases, please contact Sterling Special Sales
Department at 800-805-5489 or specialsales@sterlingpublishing.com.

SARINA JACOBSON

TEA

More than 80 Delicious Recipes

PHOTOGRAPHY BY DANYA WEINER

STERLING

New York / London
www.sterlingpublishing.com

TABLE OF CONTENTS

INTRODUCTION 6
Origins of Tea 6

Types of Tea 6

Health Benefits of Drinking Tea 9

Choosing Tea 9

Storing Tea 10

Brewing a Perfect Cup of Tea 11

Common Substitutions 13

TEATIME IN ENGLAND 14
Preparing English Tea 18

Tea Sandwiches 19

   Smoked Salmon with Ginger Butter 19

   Cucumber and Mint 20

   Goat Cheese and Watercress 20

   Egg Salad Flowers 22

   Cheddar Cheese with Chutney Butter 22

Traditional Crumpets 23

Scottish Shortbread 24

Lemon Curd 24

Honey Butter 25

Traditional Scones 25

Scone Variations 26

TEATIME IN CHINA 28
Preparing Chinese Tea 32

Chinese Almond Cookies 33

Candied Walnuts 33

Festive Fortune Cookies 34

Mango Muffins 36

TEATIME IN JAPAN 38
Preparing Japanese Tea 42

Coconut Rice Squares 42

Green Tea Loaf 44

Dorayaki 46

Japanese-Style Cheesecake 47

TEATIME IN INDIA 48
Preparing Indian Tea 52

Curried Corn Patties 52

Creamy Rice Pudding 54

Cardamom Butter Cookies 54

Walnut, Date, and Coconut Banana Loaf 55

Green Mango Chutney 55

Coconut Ladoos 56

Rava Ladoos 56

TEATIME IN RUSSIA 58
Preparing Russian Tea 62

Pecan Tea Cakes 62

Spiced Honey Cake 63

Plum Cake 64

Chocolate-Covered Strawberries 64

Blini 66

Walnut Ginger Cookies 66

TEA COOLERS 68
Sugar Syrup 71

Classic Iced Tea 71

Sweet Southern Iced Tea 71

Iced Jasmine Tea 72

Iced Spice Tea 72

Sun Tea 74

Mint Tea Punch 74

Cranberry Iced Tea Cooler 75

Iced Honey, Lime, and Ginger Tea 75

Iced Sencha Tea 76

Iced Apple and Spice Tea 76

Thai Iced Tea 78

Iced Chamomile, Lemon, and Lavender Tea 78

Flavored Frozen Tea Cubes 80

   Lemon Lime Tea Cubes 80

   Ginger and Honey Tea Cubes 80

TEA COMFORTERS 82

Chocolate Chai 85

Very Spicy Chai 85

Tea Nog 86

Kashmiri Chai 86

Hot Cider Tea 88

Milky Vanilla Tea 88

Spicy Cranberry Tea 90

Chai Latte 90

TISANES 92

Citrus Blend 95

Linden Flowers 95

Chamomile 96

Elderflower 96

Fennel 96

Rooibos 98

Peppermint 98

Ginger 98

COOKING WITH TEA 100

Tea-Smoked Salmon 103

Tea-Smoked Chicken 103

Rooibos Couscous with Snow Peas and Shitake Mushrooms 104

White Fish in Peppermint and Lemon Tea 106

Peppermint Lamb Chops 106

Creamy Potato Chamomile Soup 108

Marbled Tea Eggs 110

Chamomile-Infused White Chocolate Sauce 110

Lavender Shortbread Cookies 112

Jasmine and Citrus Pound Cake 114

Green Tea Ice Cream 116

Lavender Whipped Cream 116

HOSTING A TEA PARTY 118

Cream Cheese Tartlets 121

Mini Heart Pizzas 121

White Chocolate Mini Cakes 124

Festive Cupcakes 126

INDEX 128

INTRODUCTION

ORIGINS OF TEA

No one is really sure when the first cup of tea was brewed, but most people date it to ancient China, perhaps as early as 5,000 years ago. According to legend, the Divine Farmer discovered tea after some wild tea leaves drifted into a pot of water he was boiling outdoors.

Initially, tea was brewed by boiling tea leaves along with salt, ginger, and other ingredients. Later, it became common practice to infuse loose tea leaves with hot water, then pour the infusion into small bowls. Over time, China developed an extraordinarily sophisticated tea culture, one which eventually spread to Japan, Europe, and around the world.

TYPES OF TEA

All true teas are made from the processed leaves of the tea bush, *Camellia sinensis*, a shrub that was first domesticated in southwestern China. Today, tea is cultivated all over the world, with particularly large industries in Sri Lanka, China, and Kenya. The quality of the leaves is affected by a number of factors, including the soil in which the tea grows, the climate, and the time of picking.

There are countless varieties of tea. The largest classifications are black, green, and oolong, categories which refer to how the leaves are processed. Processing tea leaves involves a range of activities, including wilting, bruising, heating, and oxidizing. The main difference between tea varieties is how much oxygen is absorbed by the leaves during processing.

Black tea is made from leaves that have undergone a full fermentation process that includes wilting, rolling, fermenting, and drying. Black tea is allowed to oxidize for a relatively long period of time, giving it a rich herbal taste. Common Indian black teas include Assam and Darjeeling. Ceylon is a popular black tea from Sri Lanka. These teas are often served with milk and sugar.

6

Scented tea

Black tea

White tea

Green tea

Oolong tea

Green teas, also known as unfermented teas, are made from unoxidized leaves that are heated, rolled, and dried. These teas are the most common type consumed in China and Japan. Dragon Well, Gunpowder, and Green Snail Spring are some of China's most popular varieties of green tea. These teas are never served with milk.

Oolong teas are allowed to partially oxidize, giving them a rich floral flavor. The raw leaves are sun-wilted and then bruised, which exposes their juices to the air so that the leaves oxidize and brown quickly, like cut fruit. Imperial Gold, Formosa Oolong, and Iron Buddha are types of Chinese oolong tea. These teas are never served with milk.

White teas are produced on a very limited scale in China and India. They are the least processed types of tea. New tea buds are plucked before they open and simply allowed to dry. The curled-up buds have a silvery appearance and produce a pale, very delicate cup of tea. These teas are never served with milk.

Scented teas are made by mixing flavoring(s) with the tea leaves. To make jasmine tea, for example, jasmine blossoms are added to green or oolong tea. Fruit-scented teas are generally made by combining a fruit's essential oil with black tea. Earl Grey is probably the most common scented tea, made with a mixture of orange bergamot and black tea.

Tisanes, commonly called herbal teas, aren't technically teas at all, since they aren't made from the leaves of the tea bush. Tisanes are infusions made with herbal materials such as fresh or dried leaves, flowers, seeds, or roots.

Tea leaves are also classified by size. Small leaves are usually used for making tea bags, whereas large leaves are generally packaged as loose tea. The term orange pekoe, for example, classifies a large leaf size; broken orange pekoe describes a smaller leaf size.

HEALTH BENEFITS OF DRINKING TEA

Drinking hot tea is a daily ritual for millions of people. In warm climates, tea seems to dispel the heat and bring a feeling of instant cooling, together with a sense of relaxation. In cooler climates, tea is a comforting drink that warms the body and soul on cold days.

In addition to these pleasures, tea also provides a number of health benefits. It contains flavonoids, which are naturally occurring compounds believed to have antioxidant properties. Tea also includes tannic acid, a chemical known for its anti-inflammatory and germicidal properties.

Green tea offers additional benefits due to its rich content of catechin polyphenols. The most powerful of these is epigallocatechin-3, or EGCG, a substance beneficial to heart and circulatory health, and which supports the body's natural resistance to disease. EGCG is also believed to inhibit the growth of cancerous cells.

Tea made from tea leaves naturally contains caffeine, an alkaloid which acts as a nerve center stimulant, thus increasing heart rate and alertness. A cup of black tea contains about half the caffeine found in a regular cup of coffee. The same amount of green tea contains about one-quarter as much caffeine as a cup of coffee. Oolong tea is right in the middle, with slightly more than one-third of the caffeine found in coffee. Tisanes, not being brewed from tea leaves, are often caffeine-free, although this depends on what herb is infused to brew them.

CHOOSING TEA

With so many teas on the market, how do you choose what type to pour into your cup? Sampling is a great way to try out new teas before investing in a large quantity. Every tea vendor worth his leaf should offer mini samples, starter kits, or variety packs.

As for whether loose tea or tea bags are better, that's very much up to the individual. People who prefer loose tea say it brews a better cup, with more flavor and aroma than tea brewed with tea bags. Many also believe that tea bags are made with tea dust, the tiny particles of tea that fall to the ground during leaf processing. While this may or may not be true for mass-produced tea bags, it is certainly not true of high-quality tea bags. Anyway, millions of tea-lovers use tea bags every day and have no complaints about their tea. Tea bags are definitely simpler to prepare and clean up than loose: just pour boiling water over the bag, steep as instructed, and discard. Ultimately, the choice between loose tea and tea bags is one of personal preference, since excellent cups of tea can be brewed using either method.

When choosing tea, first think about the strength you are looking for to narrow down your flavor options. Sometimes it helps to think about when you will drink the tea. Do you want something strong to get you going in the morning? Are you looking for something gentler to perk you up around midday? Perhaps you want a delicate tea to help you settle down in the evening? Most teas are packaged with information that describes both strength and flavor to help you choose what's most appropriate for drinking at various times of day.

STORING TEA
Tea can preserve its flavor for a relatively long time if stored properly. Generally speaking, loose leaves will retain their flavor for up to 2 years, and tea bags can be kept for about 6 months.

Keep in an airtight container
Tea absorbs moisture easily, so store it in an airtight container, such as a sealed canister or special tea caddy. Tea caddies are canisters designed for storing loose tea leaves and tea bags. (In the past, tea caddies were equipped with locks to prevent servants from stealing the tea leaves!) Today, high-quality

tea caddies (without locks) can be found in specialty tea shops and kitchen supply stores.

Store in a dark place
Tea does not like harsh light, so store it away from direct light of any sort. Again, tea caddies are a great solution.

Keep away from odors
Tea tends to absorb odors, so storing it near the spice rack probably isn't the best idea. It can also take on cooking odors, so keep it as far as possible from your oven and stove.

Do not store tea in the refrigerator or freezer, as changes in humidity can ruin the tea.

BREWING A PERFECT CUP OF TEA

Every tea drinker has his or her own idea of what constitutes the perfect cup of tea. Some people like their tea strong, while others prefer it weak. Some people like tea with milk, others prefer it with sugar, others with milk and sugar. Of course, there are purists too: They like their tea perfectly plain.

Tea-drinking preferences can get more complicated still. Serious tea aficionados can be passionate about such details as what season the tea leaves were picked, whether the tea was steeped in a teapot or a mug, what kind of clay was used to make the teapot, what exact temperature the water was, etc.

Whatever your preferences may be, these basic considerations might help you brew a tastier tea.

Water
Regardless of the type of tea you brew, the most plentiful ingredient in your cup will be water. You can use spring, bottled, or tap water as you like. The

most important thing is to make sure you use, fresh, cold water every time. Do not re-boil water that has already boiled once, since this reduces oxygen levels and can affect the taste of the tea.

Temperature

Some people recommend using a thermometer to measure the precise temperature of the water. While this may be ideal, there are simpler options. When brewing most black teas, the water should be at a rolling boil just before you pour it over the tea. Bring the teapot to the kettle (rather than the kettle to the teapot) to ensure that the hottest water possible is in your teapot.

For most green or white teas, the water should be hot but not boiling when you pour it over the tea. Brewing these teas with boiling water can cause them to turn bitter. To brew with water before it boils, heat the water until small bubbles begin to rise from the bottom of the kettle, then pour over the tea. To brew with water after it has boiled, simply let the boiled water sit for two or three minutes, then pour it over the tea.

Preparing the vessel

Whether you drink your tea from a teapot or a mug, it's best to preheat the vessel beforehand. This prevents heat loss while the tea is steeping. Before placing tea in the vessel, simply pour in a little hot water, swirl it around, and discard.

Amount of tea

The strength of your tea depends upon the amount of tea you use, not how long the tea steeps. A general rule is to use 1 teaspoon of loose leaves or 1 tea bag for every 6 ounces of water. People who take their tea with milk often add one extra teaspoon of tea (or one extra tea bag) if they are brewing a whole pot of tea. If you are using a mesh tea ball to brew loose tea leaves, only fill the ball halfway. This leaves room for the leaves to expand as they steep.

Steeping times
Refer to the table below to decide how long to brew your tea. Be sure to remove loose leaves or tea bags before serving the tea, as letting tea steep for too long results in bitter (not stronger) tea.

Type of Tea	Water Temperature	Steeping Time
Most small-leaf black teas	Boiling	2–3 minutes
Most large-leaf black teas	Boiling	3–5 minutes
Green teas	Cooler than boiling	2–3 minutes
White teas	Cooler than boiling	5–7 minutes
Tisanes	Boiling	10–20 minutes

COMMON SUBSTITUTIONS
Many of the recipes in this book call for tea. Tea bags and loose leaves are interchangeable in every recipe. To substitute bags for leaves, use 1 tea bag for each teaspoon of leaves called for. To substitute leaves for tea bags, use 1 teaspoon for each tea bag called for.

When substituting loose leaves for tea bags, strain the tea by pouring it through a fine mesh strainer or a piece of cheesecloth into your drinking or serving vessel. In some cases, it may be convenient to "bind" the leaves for easy removal later. In such a case, use a tea ball (or multiple teaballs, to give large quantities of tea plenty of room to expand), or wrap your leaves in a piece of cheesecloth and tie with cooking string before steeping.

Of course, if you don't have a teapot for steeping your tea, you may substitute with a heatproof bowl, pot, or pitcher with a lid.

13

TEATIME IN ENGLAND

Tea was introduced to England via Holland in the mid-seventeenth century, several years after being introduced to mainland Europe. Although it was initially enjoyed only by the upper classes, tea soon became England's most popular beverage. According to legend, it was Anna, the seventh Duchess of Bedford, who began the afternoon tea ritual sometime in the early nineteenth century. The duchess asked for tea and light refreshments in her room one afternoon, and enjoyed the experience so much that she started inviting friends to join her.

The practice was quickly picked up by other ladies of society, and before long, attending elegant tea parties was extremely fashionable. The standard menu at these affairs included small cakes, bread and butter sandwiches, assorted sweets, and of course, tea. Over time, the menu expanded to include wafer-thin, crustless sandwiches, fish paté, toasted breads with jams, and traditional British pastries such as scones and crumpets.

Two distinct forms of tea service soon evolved: Low Tea and High Tea. Low Tea was served in the early part of the afternoon in wealthy, aristocratic homes. It featured gourmet tidbits rather than solid meals. There was lots of tea, of course, but the emphasis was on presentation and conversation. High Tea, also known as Meat Tea, became the main meal of the day for the middle and lower classes. Served in the late afternoon, it consisted of nourishing foods such as roast beef, mashed potatoes, cooked vegetables, and of course, tea.

The popularity of formal tea waned as lifestyles changed, but the tradition is enjoying a revival today, as more people yearn for the distinct elegance associated with sitting down to sip tea and chat. Formal tea is once again served in hotels, restaurants, and cafés, and many people have begun to hold English-style tea parties in their homes.

PREPARING ENGLISH TEA

English tea is generally prepared with black tea blends such as English Breakfast or Irish Breakfast, or with scented tea such as Earl Grey.

PREPARATION

1. Preheat your teapot first. To do this, pour in a little hot water, swirl it around, and discard. By warming your vessel in advance, you ensure that the temperature of the water you pour in later won't take a sudden, drastic drop.

2. Place the tea in the vessel. Use 1 heaping teaspoon of loose tea or 1 tea bag for every 6 ounces of water. Add an extra 1 heaping teaspoon of loose leaves or an extra bag "for the pot," as the English say. If you prefer your tea stronger (or weaker), add more (or less) tea.

3. Bring the water to a rolling boil and pour immediately over the tea. Don't let the water boil too long, and don't let it cool before pouring over the tea.

4. Cover the teapot and let the tea steep for 3 to 5 minutes. Don't steep for too long, as this will make the tea taste bitter.

5. Pour the tea into cups and add milk, sugar, or both, as desired.

Tea Sandwiches

Bite-size sandwiches are a distinctive English teatime treat. To make them just right, the bread must be sliced very thin, and the crust should be removed. Many bakeries can slice bread extra thin on request. If you are slicing the bread yourself, freeze it partially in advance and use a sharp, serrated knife for slicing. Make the slices even thinner by rolling them gently with a rolling pin before spreading on the filling. To serve, arrange the sandwiches on a bed of crisp iceberg lettuce. The lettuce makes an attractive background and keeps the sandwiches moist. Wrap the serving tray tightly with plastic wrap and refrigerate until ready to serve.

SMOKED SALMON WITH GINGER BUTTER

This sandwich features the classic trio of pumpernickel, cream cheese, and smoked salmon.

INGREDIENTS

Makes 12 open-faced sandwiches

½ cup unsalted butter, softened

4 ounces cream cheese, room temperature

1 teaspoon grated fresh ginger

1 tablespoon freshly squeezed lime juice, plus more for garnish

3 tablespoons chopped fresh cilantro

12 thin slices pumpernickel bread

12 thin slices smoked salmon

PREPARATION

1. In a food processor, mix together butter, cream cheese, ginger, lime juice, and cilantro just until combined. Transfer to an airtight container and refrigerate at least 1 hour to let the flavors blend.

2. Use a large, round cookie cutter to cut perfect circles out of each slice of bread.

3. Spread a generous layer of butter mixture on each circle, lay a slice of salmon on top, sprinkle with scallion slices, and drizzle with a little lime juice.

19

CUCUMBER AND MINT

To make the cucumber slices really thin, try using a vegetable peeler.

INGREDIENTS

Serves 4 to 8

2 tablespoons butter, softened

2 tablespoons finely chopped fresh mint

8 thin slices white bread, crust removed

2 small cucumbers, peeled and sliced into very thin rounds

PREPARATION

1. In a small bowl, mix together butter and mint until well combined.

2. Spread a thin layer of butter mixture onto each slice of bread.

3. Arrange cucumber slices on four of the buttered bread slices and top with the other four to make sandwiches.

4. Cut sandwiches into triangles or squares, or use a round cookie cutter to cut out perfect circles.

GOAT CHEESE AND WATERCRESS

Stimulate your taste buds with this interesting combination of pecans, watercress, and goat cheese.

INGREDIENTS

Makes 8 open-faced sandwiches

8 thin slices brown bread

12 ounces soft goat cheese

1 cup chopped fresh watercress

¾ cup finely chopped toasted pecans

Salt and freshly ground black pepper

PREPARATION

1. Use a large, heart-shaped cookie cutter to cut a heart out of each slice of bread.

2. Thinly spread goat cheese on each heart. Arrange watercress on top and sprinkle with pecans. Add salt and pepper to taste.

Clockwise from front left:
Goat Cheese and Watercress (1st and 4th), Egg Salad Flowers (2nd and 5th),
Cucumber and Mint (3rd and 6th)

EGG SALAD FLOWERS

*Add a floral touch to your sandwich platter
(see photo, page 21).*

INGREDIENTS

*Makes 12 open-faced
sandwiches*

6 large hard-boiled
eggs, peeled and
chopped

3 tablespoons
mayonnaise, plus more
for spreading

1 tablespoon sour
cream

1 small cucumber,
peeled and chopped

3 tablespoons chopped
fresh chives

Salt and freshly ground
black pepper

12 thin slices white
bread

Chive blossoms or
watercress sprigs for
garnish

PREPARATION

1. In a medium bowl,
mix together eggs,
mayonnaise, and sour
cream. Fold in cucumber
and chives. Add salt and
pepper to taste.

2. Thinly spread
mayonnaise on each slice
of bread, then spread a
thin layer of egg mixture
on top.

3. Use a large, flower-
shaped cookie cutter to
cut each slice of bread
into a flower.

4. Garnish by arranging
chive blossoms or
watercress sprigs in a
circle at the center of each
sandwich.

CHEDDAR CHEESE WITH CHUTNEY BUTTER

*Add a flavor of India to your table at teatime with this
lively combination of curry, chutney, and pickled gherkins.*

INGREDIENTS

Serves 4 to 8

½ cup salted butter,
softened

¼ teaspoon curry
powder

3 tablespoons mango or
peach chutney

2 cups grated cheddar
cheese

½ cup diced pickled
gherkins

½ cup chopped arugula

8 thin slices rye bread,
crust removed

PREPARATION

1. In a small bowl, mix
together butter, curry
powder, and chutney.

2. In a separate bowl, use
a fork to toss together
cheese, gherkins, and
arugula.

3. Thinly spread butter
mixture onto each bread
slice.

4. Sprinkle cheese mixture
onto four of the slices,
then top with the other
four to make sandwiches.

5. Cut sandwiches into
triangles or squares, or
use a round cookie cutter
to cut out perfect circles.

22

TRADITIONAL CRUMPETS

Enjoy this traditional treat with a thick layer of honey butter (see recipe, page 25).

INGREDIENTS

Makes 18 crumpets

4 cups sifted all-purpose flour

½ teaspoon salt

1 teaspoon sugar

2 teaspoons active dry yeast

1¼ cups whole milk

1¼ cups water

Butter for greasing

Vegetable oil for frying

PREPARATION

1. In a large bowl, mix together flour and salt. Stir in sugar and yeast.

2. In a small saucepan over low heat, heat milk and water until warm. Make a well in the center of the flour mixture, pour in milk mixture, and mix until a thick batter forms. Cover with a kitchen towel and set aside to rise in a warm place about 1 hour, until batter has a light springy texture.

3. Generously grease four crumpet rings (or 3-inch round cookie cutters) with butter.

4. Stir risen batter to remove air pockets and pour into a large pitcher. Heat a nonstick frying pan over low heat. Add a drop of oil to pan and spread evenly over surface with a paper towel, removing excess. Place greased crumpet rings in pan and continue heating for about 2 minutes.

5. Pour batter into rings until half full. Cook about 10 minutes, until small holes appear on the surface of each crumpet and the top is dry.

6. Use an oven glove or kitchen towel to remove the hot rings, then turn over crumpets and cook another 1 to 2 minutes. Transfer to a wire rack to cool slightly. Serve warm.

SCOTTISH SHORTBREAD

Served with lemon curd (see recipe, this page), this cookie makes a filling Scottish treat.

INGREDIENTS

Makes 16 cookies

1½ cups all-purpose flour

¾ cup cornstarch

⅛ teaspoon salt

½ cup plus 2 tablespoons superfine (castor) sugar

1 cup unsalted butter, cold

1 teaspoon pure vanilla extract

PREPARATION

1. Preheat oven to 300°F and position a rack in the middle of the oven. Line an 8 × 2-inch square cake pan with heavy aluminum foil, allowing the foil to extend over two sides of the pan, forming a "sling" with which you'll lift the shortbread out after baking.

2. Sift together flour, cornstarch, and salt. Mix in ½ cup sugar.

3. Cut in butter, add vanilla, and mix about 2 minutes, until mixture resembles coarse crumbs.

4. Gently press dough into prepared pan. Bake 70 minutes, until top is golden. Sprinkle with remaining 2 tablespoons sugar. Cut into squares while warm, taking care to cut all the way through to the foil. Let cool completely before lifting the foil to remove the shortbread.

LEMON CURD

This refreshing topping should be served chilled, and is even better prepared a day or two in advance.

INGREDIENTS

Makes 1½ cups

6 tablespoons unsalted butter, softened

1 cup sugar

2 large free-range eggs

2 large free-range egg yolks

⅔ cup freshly squeezed lemon juice

1 teaspoon grated lemon zest

PREPARATION

1. Cream together butter and sugar. Gradually add eggs and egg yolks while beating, and continue to beat another minute, until blended. Mix in lemon juice.

2. Transfer mixture to a heavy saucepan over low heat. (The mixture will look curdled, but don't worry, it smoothes out as it cooks.) When butter has melted and mixture is smooth, increase heat to medium and cook 15 minutes, stirring constantly, until thickened. Don't let the mixture boil.

3. Remove from heat, stir in lemon zest, and transfer to a bowl. Cover with plastic wrap, taking care to press wrap directly onto the surface of the curd, which prevents a skin from forming. Transfer to refrigerator and chill until firm, at least 1 hour. Serve chilled.

HONEY BUTTER

This sweet butter is lovely on crispy toast, fresh bread, or warm crumpets (see recipe, page 23).

INGREDIENTS

Makes 2 cups

2 cups butter, softened

¼ cup honey

¼ teaspoon ground cinnamon

¼ teaspoon ground nutmeg

½ teaspoon pure vanilla extract

PREPARATION

1. With an electric mixer, beat butter at low speed until loosened. Increase speed to medium, add honey, cinnamon, nutmeg, and vanilla, and beat until well combined.

2. Transfer butter to a piece of parchment paper and roll into a log. Refrigerate at least 2 hours. To serve, unwrap parchment paper and slice log into disks.

TRADITIONAL SCONES

Often served with clotted cream, these pastries are also lovely with fresh marmalade and creamy butter.

INGREDIENTS

Makes 12 to 16 scones

2 cups all-purpose flour, plus more for dusting

1 tablespoon baking powder

2 tablespoons sugar

½ teaspoon salt

3 tablespoons butter, cold

1 large free-range egg, beaten

½–¾ cup whole milk

PREPARATION

1. Preheat oven to 450°F and line a baking sheet with parchment paper.

2. In a medium bowl, sift together flour, baking powder, sugar, and salt.

3. Cut in butter until mixture resembles coarse crumbs. Set aside some of the egg for brushing on top later, and stir in the rest.

4. Gradually add milk, stirring until a thick dough forms.

5. On a lightly floured surface, knead dough, then roll out to ½ inch thick. Use a 1-inch, round cookie cutter to cut out scones, and arrange them on the prepared baking sheet. Brush tops with the remaining beaten egg. Bake 15 to 20 minutes, until golden brown.

SCONE VARIATIONS

*To create delicious teatime snacks that are spicy, savory, or sweet, follow
the recipe for Traditional Scones (see recipe, page 25), and make the
following alterations.*

SPICED SCONES

Mix together a pinch each of
ground cinnamon, ground
nutmeg, ground cloves, and
ground allspice for a total of
¼ teaspoon, and add with flour
to dry ingredients in step 1.

BUTTERMILK SCONES

Increase sugar to 3 tablespoons
and replace whole milk with
buttermilk.

WALNUT SCONES

Mix in ¾ cup chopped walnuts
with the flour.

CHEDDAR CHEESE AND
CHIVE SCONES

Toss together 1 cup grated
cheddar cheese, ⅛ teaspoon
dry mustard powder, and
2 tablespoons chopped chives,
and add with the milk.

DRIED FRUIT SCONES

Toss together dried currants,
dried cranberries, and dried
apricots for a total of ½ cup,
and add with the flour.

CITRUS SCONES

Mix together 1 tablespoon
sugar with the juice and zest of
1 lemon or orange, and add with
the milk.

DOUBLE CHOCOLATE
SCONES

Add ¼ cup cocoa powder, ⅓ cup
semisweet chocolate chips, and
⅓ cup white chocolate chips to
dry ingredients in step 1. Replace
milk with heavy cream and add
1 teaspoon pure vanilla extract in
step 3.

WHOLE-WHEAT RAISIN
SCONES

Replace 1 cup of all-purpose flour
with 1 cup whole-wheat flour,
replace sugar with brown sugar,
and replace whole milk with
buttermilk. Add ½ cup raisins to
dry ingredients in step 1.

Opposite: Scone Variations

TEATIME IN CHINA

Tea was discovered in China, so it's no surprise that tea-drinking plays an important role in Chinese culture. An ancient Chinese proverb even claims: "Better to be deprived of food for three days than of tea for one." In China, tea has inspired poetry and songs, and cemented lifelong friendships. The ritual of preparing and serving tea holds a special place in the hearts and minds of people from many diverse populations in Chinese society, from aristocrats to intellectuals, poets, farmers, and businesspeople.

The art of making tea in China is called *cha dao*. It involves a preparation ceremony that uses several specialized utensils. Each server performs the ritual in his or her own way, as every step in the process is meant to be an individual sensory exploration of the beverage. Even the folding of the napkin is done according to tradition, and is said to ward off bad *qi* energy.

Serving tea is a sign of respect, and there are several circumstances in which tea ceremonies are held specifically for this purpose. Younger people may offer their elders tea during an informal visit. Large family gatherings often include the ceremonial drinking of tea, and it's not uncommon for extended families to gather in large restaurants to have tea. People may make serious apologies to others by pouring them tea. At a traditional Chinese marriage ceremony, the bride and groom kneel in front of their parents and serve them tea. In addition to being consumed on such casual and formal occasions, tea is also used in traditional Chinese medicine and in Chinese cuisine.

Most of the tea used in Chinese tea ceremonies is grown in the mountains of Taiwan. The tea is lightly fermented and particularly refined. It is steeped for very short periods of time in a small, unglazed clay teapot, then transferred to small matching cups. Tiny cups that hold no more than two sips of tea are particularly popular in southern coastal China; larger cups are more common in busy cities such as Shanghai and Beijing.

PREPARING CHINESE TEA

*Chinese tea is generally prepared with green teas such as Dragon Well,
Gunpowder, or Green Snail Spring.*

PREPARATION

1. Preheat your teapot by pouring in a little hot water, swirling it around, and discarding. By warming your teapot in advance, you ensure that the temperature of the water you pour in later won't take a sudden, drastic drop. Place the teacups close together on your table.

2. Using chopsticks or a bamboo tea scoop, pick up the tea leaves and place them in the teapot. (Use about 1 teaspoon of loose green tea leaves for every ¾ cup of water.) Pour in a little hot water to rinse the leaves, then immediately pour the water back out, leaving only the soaked leaves behind.

3. Heat the water until bubbles start to rise from the bottom of the kettle. Do not let the water boil. Hold the teapot over a large bowl and pour the water from the kettle into the teapot. Continue pouring water even after the pot is full, allowing the overflow to run into the bowl.

4. Cover the teapot and let the tea steep for about 30 seconds.

5. Pour the tea into the teacups by moving the teapot around in a continual circular motion, filling all the cups at the same time. The goal is for the tea in each cup to taste exactly the same.

6. Distribute the tea to your guests. When you are ready for the next round of tea, heat fresh water almost to boiling and pour it into the teapot. Let it steep for a little longer this time (about 40 seconds). Gather the cups together again and pour the tea into them with the same circular motion.

7. Repeat the process as many as 3 or 4 times with the same leaves, allowing the tea to steep a little longer each time. The goal is to make each round of tea—and each cup of tea—taste exactly the same.

CHINESE ALMOND COOKIES

These cookies have a rich, nutty flavor.

INGREDIENTS

Makes 24 cookies

1 cup cake flour, plus more for dusting

¾ cup confectioners' sugar

¼ teaspoon salt

½ cup finely ground blanched almonds

6 tablespoons nut oil (such as peanut, walnut, or almond)

1 large free-range egg, well beaten

1 teaspoon almond extract

24 whole blanched almonds

Vegetable oil for greasing

PREPARATION

1. Preheat oven to 375°F. Grease a baking sheet with vegetable oil.

2. In a large bowl, sift together flour, confectioners' sugar, salt, and ground almonds. Stir in oil, egg, and almond extract, mixing gently until a soft dough forms.

3. On a lightly floured surface, roll out dough to about ¼ inch thick. Cut out cookies using a 1-inch round cookie cutter and arrange on prepared baking sheet. Press a blanched almond into the center of each cookie. Bake about 15 minutes, or until golden. Transfer to a wire rack to cool.

CANDIED WALNUTS

Great on their own, these sweet nuts are perfect for garnishing cakes, cookies, or ice cream.

INGREDIENTS

Makes 2 pounds

2 pounds walnut halves

1 cup sugar

2 teaspoons ground cinnamon

¼ teaspoon salt

6 tablespoons whole milk

1 teaspoon pure vanilla extract

PREPARATION

1. Preheat oven to 350°F. Line a baking sheet with parchment paper.

2. Spread walnuts in single layer on lined baking sheet and roast 8 to 10 minutes, until brown and fragrant. Set aside to cool, then transfer to a large bowl.

3. In a medium saucepan over medium heat, stir together sugar, cinnamon, salt, and milk, and cook about 8 minutes, until mixture thickens. Remove from heat and stir in vanilla. Pour over walnuts and mix to coat.

4. Spread coated nuts out on a clean piece of parchment paper, separating clumps with a fork. Cool completely before serving.

FESTIVE
FORTUNE COOKIES

With these colorful cookies at your tea party, your good fortune is guaranteed!

INGREDIENTS

Makes 35 cookies

One ½ pound bag Chinese fortune cookies

3½ ounces white chocolate, coarsely chopped

3½ ounces bittersweet chocolate, coarsely chopped

Colored sprinkles

Crushed nuts

PREPARATION

1. Remove fortune cookies from wrappers and set aside.

2. Melt white chocolate in the top of a double boiler and transfer to a small bowl. Melt bittersweet chocolate in the top of a double boiler and transfer to a small bowl. (If you're using the same top pot in your double boiler, be sure to clean it in between meltings so as not to fade the color of the brown chocolate.)

3. Dip the top of half of the cookies in white chocolate. Dip the top of the other half in bittersweet chocolate.

4. Decorate the cookies in a variety of ways: Pipe bittersweet chocolate on some of the white chocolate cookies, and vice versa, or decorate with colored sprinkles and crushed nuts.

MANGO MUFFINS

With their subtle sweetness, these muffins are perfect alongside unsweetened green tea.

INGREDIENTS

Makes 12 muffins

2½ cups self-rising flour

¾ cup superfine (castor) sugar

1 free-range egg, beaten lightly

1 teaspoon pure vanilla extract

¼ teaspoon ground cinnamon

⅓ cup vegetable oil

½ cup buttermilk

½ cup coconut cream

2 ripe mangoes, peeled, pitted, and chopped

2 tablespoons honey

PREPARATION

1. Preheat oven to 400°F. Line a 12-cup muffin pan with paper liners.

2. In a large bowl, sift together flour and sugar. Stir in egg, vanilla, cinnamon, oil, buttermilk, coconut cream, mangoes, and honey, and mix until combined.

3. Divide batter evenly among muffin cups and bake about 20 minutes, until golden. Let cool in pan 5 minutes, then remove from pan to a wire rack, right side up. Let cool completely.

TEATIME IN JAPAN

Tea was introduced to Japan from China sometime during the ninth century. The development of the Japanese tea ceremony, a formal tea-drinking experience, occurred some time later, likely during the fifteenth century. The first Tea Master was a Zen priest named Murata Shuko. Since then, there have been many Tea Masters and countless students of the Japanese tea ceremony, all striving to make it as elegant and graceful as possible.

There is a wide variety of Japanese tea ceremonies, and they differ greatly, yet all of them focus on celebrating beauty and the mundane aspects of life. In addition to tea, the ceremonies may involve decorative flowers, artwork, calligraphy, or food.

Both the host and the guests in the ceremony have roles to fulfill. The host usually dresses in a kimono, and guests wait in a garden or courtyard until summoned. After a ritual hand-washing, guests enter the room where the ceremony will be held. This room is often decorated with a hanging scroll or floral arrangement. Guests are expected to admire the decorations while they wait, and may be offered a light meal or snack before the ceremony begins.

At all types of ceremonies, several specialized utensils are used to prepare the tea. These include a tea scoop, a whisk, tea bowls, and special cloths to clean the utensils before and after use. The host begins the formal procedure of preparing the tea while guests look on. Conversation is kept at a minimum, and guests enjoy the sights, smells, and sounds of the process.

Once prepared, the tea is first served to the guest of honor. This guest exchanges bows with the host, lifts the bowl in a sign of respect, rotates the bowl, and takes three sips of tea. He then wipes the rim of the bowl, rotates it again, and passes it to the second guest with a bow. The second guest performs the same ritual as the first, and so on until all the guests have had tea and the bowl is returned to the host.

The host carefully cleans the utensils according to ritual, and the utensils are then admired by the guest of honor, followed by the rest of the guests. All guests treat the utensils with great respect and care. The host then gathers the utensils and bids farewell to his guests.

PREPARING JAPANESE TEA

Powdered green tea known as matcha *is used to make Japanese tea. Common Japanese tea varieties include* sencha, gyokuro, *and* genmaicha.

PREPARATION

1. Preheat your tea bowl or wide-rimmed cup by pouring in a little warm water, swirling it around, and discarding. Dry the bowl thoroughly with a clean cloth.

2. Use a tea scoop to measure ½ teaspoon *matcha* green tea powder into the bowl or cup.

3. Heat the water until bubbles begin to rise from the bottom of the kettle. Do not let the water boil. Pour ¼ cup of hot water over the tea powder.

4. Stir the tea with a whisk, starting slowly and gradually increasing the speed until the tea takes on a foamy consistency.

5. The tea may be served in a single tea bowl from which everyone drinks, or in individual tea bowls.

COCONUT RICE SQUARES

Using sticky sushi rice in this recipe is the trick to making the rice stay together.

INGREDIENTS

Makes 24 squares

4 cups cooked sushi rice

1 cup sugar

1 teaspoon baking powder

¼ teaspoon salt

½ cup whole milk

1 cup coconut cream

1 cup flaked coconut

2 large free-range eggs

1 teaspoon pure vanilla extract

½ teaspoon rose extract or
1 teaspoon rose water

PREPARATION

1. Preheat oven to 350°F and position a rack in the middle of the oven. Line a 4 × 8-inch baking pan with parchment paper.

2. In a large bowl, gently toss together rice, sugar, baking powder, and salt. In a separate large bowl, whisk together the milk, coconut cream, flaked coconut, eggs, vanilla extract, and rose extract. Pour liquid mixture into dry mixture and stir until well combined.

3. Pour batter into prepared pan and level top with a spatula. Bake 1 to 1½ hours, until top is golden and center is firm. Let cool completely in pan before cutting into squares to serve.

GREEN TEA LOAF

With its lovely green hue, this loaf is as pleasing to the eye as it is to the palate.

INGREDIENTS

Makes one 8½ × 4½-inch loaf

½ cup butter, softened

⅔ cup sugar

2 large free-range eggs, whisked

½ cup coconut milk

1 cup flour

1 tablespoon green tea powder

1 teaspoon baking powder

3 tablespoons chocolate chips (optional)

PREPARATION

1. Preheat oven to 325°F. Line an 8½ × 4½ × 2½-inch loaf pan with parchment paper.

2. Cream together butter and sugar. Add eggs and coconut milk, and beat until combined.

3. In a separate bowl, sift together flour, green tea powder, and baking powder.

4. Add flour mixture to egg mixture and blend until smooth. Stir in chocolate chips. Pour batter into prepared pan and bake 30 to 40 minutes, until golden brown. Let cool in pan.

DORAYAKI

These pancake sandwiches are a traditional Japanese dessert.

INGREDIENTS

Makes 10 to 12 dorayaki

Bean paste:

1 cup adzuki beans, soaked overnight

4 cups water, for boiling

¾ cup sugar

¼ teaspoon salt

Pancakes:

2 large free-range eggs

½ cup sugar

1 tablespoon honey

1 cup all-purpose flour, sifted

½ teaspoon baking powder

¼ to ½ cup water

Vegetable oil for frying

PREPARATION

1. Prepare the bean paste: Drain soaked beans and rinse with fresh water.

2. In a large saucepan over high heat, bring water to a boil. Add beans, return to boil, then reduce heat to medium-high and cook partially covered about 1½ hours, or until soft. Skim off foam as it rises.

3. Transfer beans to a colander, rinse in cold water, and return to cooking pot. Mash together beans, sugar, and salt, and heat over medium heat for about 5 minutes. Set aside to cool. (You'll have about 2 cups of bean paste.)

4. Prepare the pancakes: In a large bowl, whisk together eggs, sugar, and honey until well combined. Add flour, baking powder, and 1½ cups of the bean paste. Slowly mix in water until mixture forms a smooth batter.

5. In a large nonstick frying pan over medium-high heat, heat a teaspoon of oil until a drop of batter sizzles on contact. Drop tablespoons of batter into the pan, about 1 inch apart. Fry pancakes about 2 minutes, until the tops start to bubble. Flip over and fry other side until golden, about 1 or 2 minutes. Transfer to a plate lined with paper towels to absorb excess oil. Repeat, frying in batches, until no batter remains.

6. To serve, spread half of the pancakes with remaining bean paste and top with other half to make sandwiches.

JAPANESE-STYLE CHEESECAKE

Light and fluffy, this dessert has more in common with a soufflé than a typical cheesecake.

INGREDIENTS

Makes one 7-inch round cake

Cheesecake:

7 ounces cream cheese, room temperature

¼ cup whole milk

½ cup superfine (castor) sugar

3 large free-range eggs, separated

3 tablespoons cornstarch

2 tablespoons freshly squeezed lemon juice

½ teaspoon cream of tartar

Glaze:

2 tablespoons apricot jam

½ tablespoon water

PREPARATION

1. Prepare the cheesecake: Preheat oven to 350°F and position the rack in the bottom third of the oven. Line the bottom of a 7-inch round cake pan with parchment paper, and prepare a large roasting pan.

2. In a medium bowl, stir together cream cheese and milk. Add ¼ cup of the sugar and all of the egg yolks, cornstarch, lemon juice, and cream of tartar. Mix well.

3. In the bowl of an electric mixer, beat egg whites until soft peaks form. Add remaining ¼ cup sugar in batches, beating constantly until stiff peaks form.

4. Gently fold egg white mixture into cream cheese mixture until thoroughly combined. Transfer batter to prepared cake pan and level surface with a spatula.

5. Pour boiling water into roasting pan until about ¼ full. Carefully place the cake pan in the roasting pan, taking care not to splash water onto the batter. Bake 35 to 40 minutes, until golden. (Check cake after 20 minutes: If the surface is beginning to darken, cover with a piece of foil.) Cool cake in the pan.

6. Prepare the glaze: In a small saucepan over low heat, bring jam and water to a simmer and cook while stirring until syrupy. Let cool a few minutes before spreading on top of cooled cake. Refrigerate until ready to serve.

TEATIME
IN INDIA

Chai masala is the name for the distinct tea that has been consumed in India for generations. Recently, chai masala made its way into teacups and mugs across North America and Europe. *Chai* is the word used for tea across Asia; *masala* is the word used in India to refer to any mixture of spices. Chai masala is a warm, milky, spicy tea, traditionally served in clay cups called *kullarhs.*

Tea was first cultivated in India in the nineteenth century, when Britains looking for a place to grow tea outside of China planted Chinese tea seeds in India's Assam region. A local variety of the plant—the only variety of tea that naturally grows outside of China—was soon discovered, however, and tea from the local variety proved far tastier than the imported plant. Now, tea is one of India's main exports, and the country is second only to China in worldwide production of tea for international consumption.

Of course, tea has also become India's favorite drink. Chai masala is everywhere there: sold by vendors in the streets and in train and bus stations, and of course served in people's homes, where most families have their own unique, traditional recipe for the drink. These recipes differ vastly, but most include (among other ingredients) black tea, cardamom, ginger, cinnamon, cloves, and pepper. Most people in India drink four cups of chai masala every day. Afternoon breaks usually include a cup of chai masala served with a variety of fried savory snacks.

PREPARING INDIAN TEA

Chai masala is generally made with black Assam tea and a variety of spices.

PREPARATION

1. To prepare two cups of chai masala, use a mortar and pestle to crush together: 2 cardamom pods, 2 teaspoons grated fresh ginger, 2 or 3 whole black peppercorns, and 2 cinnamon sticks.

2. In a medium saucepan, combine 1½ cups water, ⅔ cup whole milk, and 2 teaspoons loose black tea (or 2 black tea bags) with the ground spices and bring to a boil over high heat. Boil for 1 minute, then reduce heat to very low and simmer, stirring occasionally, for about 15 minutes.

3. Pour chai masala through a fine mesh strainer into cups. Add sugar to taste and serve immediately.

CURRIED CORN PATTIES

These patties are colorful and flavorful. Serve with a refreshing chutney such as green mango chutney (see recipe, page 55).

INGREDIENTS

Makes about 6 patties

2 cups cooked corn

½ cup green beans, trimmed and chopped

2 tablespoons chopped fresh cilantro

2 large free-range eggs, beaten

¼ cup grated yellow cheese

¼ cup soft white cheese (such as cottage, cream, or ricotta)

4 tablespoons chickpea or rice flour

4 tablespoons all-purpose flour

1 teaspoon salt

2 tablespoons Indian curry paste

1 tablespoon light brown sugar

Vegetable oil for frying

PREPARATION

1. In a large bowl, mix together corn, green beans, cilantro, eggs, and cheeses. In a separate bowl, mix together flours, salt, curry paste, and brown sugar. Add flour mixture to corn mixture and stir until well combined.

2. In a large non-stick frying pan over medium heat, heat a teaspoon of oil until a drop of batter sizzles on contact. Drop tablespoons of batter into the pan about an inch apart and gently press with a spatula to flatten. Fry about 2 minutes, until brown on top. Flip patties and fry other side until brown.

3. Transfer to a plate lined with paper towels to absorb excess oil. Continue frying in batches until no batter remains. Serve warm.

CREAMY RICE PUDDING

Spice up this quintessential comfort food with cardamom and sweeten it with raisins.

INGREDIENTS

Makes 4 cups

1 cup cooked basmati or long grain rice

1 cup whole milk

½ cup heavy cream

¾ cup coconut milk

¼ cup sugar

¼ teaspoon ground cardamom

⅓ cup golden raisins

⅓ cup chopped unsalted pistachios

2 drops rose extract or 1 teaspoon rose water

PREPARATION

1. In a large saucepan over medium heat, bring rice and milk just to scalding point. Reduce heat to low and simmer, stirring constantly, about 5 minutes, until mixture begins to thicken.

2. Increase heat to medium, and stir in heavy cream, coconut milk, sugar, and cardamom. Cook for 8 to 10 minutes, until mixture begins to thicken again. Whisk periodically to prevent cardamom from clumping.

3. Remove from heat and stir in raisins, pistachios, and rose extract. Pour into individual serving bowls or a single large bowl. Cover with plastic wrap, taking care to press wrap directly onto the surface of the pudding, which prevents a skin from forming. Serve chilled or at room temperature.

CARDAMOM BUTTER COOKIES

This is a spicy twist on a traditional favorite.

INGREDIENTS

Makes 20 cookies

1 cup unsalted butter

2 cups sugar

2 teaspoons ground cardamom

4 large free-range eggs

2 cups all-purpose flour

1 teaspoon salt

PREPARATION

1. Preheat oven to 325°F. Line a baking sheet with parchment paper.

2. In a large bowl, beat butter, sugar, and cardamom until smooth and creamy. Add eggs one at a time and continue beating until well combined.

3. In a separate bowl, sift together flour and salt. Add egg mixture to flour mixture and gently combine using your hands, until a soft dough forms.

4. Drop dough by tablespoon onto prepared baking sheet, ½ inch apart. Bake 10 to 12 minutes, until golden. Transfer to a wire rack to cool before serving.

WALNUT, DATE, AND COCONUT BANANA LOAF

This loaf is full of energy and flavor.

INGREDIENTS

Makes one 8½ × 4½-inch loaf

1½ cups sugar

½ cup butter, plus more for greasing

2 large free-range eggs

1½ cups all-purpose flour

½ teaspoon baking soda

¼ teaspoon baking powder

¼ teaspoon ground cinnamon

3 large ripe bananas, mashed

1 teaspoon pure vanilla extract

½ cup chopped walnuts

¼ cup flaked coconut

¼ cup chopped pitted dates

PREPARATION

1. Preheat oven to 350°F. Grease an 8½ × 4½ × 2½-inch loaf pan with butter.

2. In a large bowl, beat sugar, butter, and eggs until blended. In a separate bowl, sift together flour, baking soda, baking powder, and cinnamon.

3. Fold flour mixture into egg mixture, followed by bananas, vanilla, walnuts, coconut, and dates.

4. Pour batter into prepared pan and bake 50 to 60 minutes, until a toothpick inserted in the center comes out clean. Cool in the pan completely before slicing.

GREEN MANGO CHUTNEY

With its surprising combination of flavors, this sweet and spicy condiment is everything a chutney should be.

INGREDIENTS

Makes 4 cups

3 green mangoes, peeled, pitted, and thinly sliced

2 cloves garlic, thinly sliced

2 teaspoons grated fresh ginger

½ cup water

2½ cups sugar

1 cup vinegar

1 teaspoon red chili powder

¾ teaspoon ground cardamom

4 teaspoons salt

4 teaspoons raisins

PREPARATION

1. In a medium saucepan over low heat, stir together mango, garlic, ginger, and water and cook until mango is tender, about 10 to 15 minutes. Add sugar, vinegar, chili powder, cardamom, and salt and continue to heat, stirring constantly, about 10 minutes, until mixture thickens and turns golden.

2. Remove from heat and mix in raisins. Let cool to room temperature, then transfer to an airtight container and refrigerate until ready to serve.

COCONUT LADOOS

These sweet balls are often served at festivals and special events.

INGREDIENTS

Makes 12 to 15 ladoos

One 14-ounce can condensed milk

2¾ cups flaked coconut

¼ teaspoon ground cardamom

1 tablespoon sugar

6 tablespoons chopped pistachios

PREPARATION

1. In a large bowl, combine condensed milk, 2 cups coconut, cardamom, and sugar.

2. Transfer to a small saucepan over low heat and cook, stirring constantly, until thickened, about 4 minutes.

3. Remove from heat and set aside to cool. Mix together the remaining ¾ cups flaked coconut with the pistachios and pour onto a large plate.

4. Shape the cooled mixture into 1-inch balls and roll in the pistachio mixture. Serve immediately or refrigerate until ready to serve.

RAVA LADOOS

These balls are made with semolina (called rava *in India) rather than regular flour, and with* ghee, *the clarified butter common in India. Both can be found in specialty food stores.*

INGREDIENTS

Makes 12 to 15 ladoos

1½ cups semolina

1 cup plus 2 tablespoons ghee

1½ cups sugar

¼ teaspoon ground cardamom

2 tablespoons finely chopped cashews

2 tablespoons raisins

PREPARATION

1. Preheat oven to 375°F. Line a baking sheet with parchment paper.

2. In a medium bowl, mix together semolina and the 2 tablespoons of ghee. Spread onto prepared baking sheet and cook until golden, about 8 minutes. Set aside to cool.

3. Transfer cooled semolina to a large bowl. Mix in sugar and cardamom.

4. In a medium saucepan over low heat, heat remaining 1 cup of ghee for about 2 minutes. Add cashews and raisins and cook until mixture thickens, about 2 more minutes.

5. Remove from heat and pour into semolina mixture. Set aside to cool slightly, then shape into 1-inch balls. Serve immediately, or refrigerate until ready to serve.

Opposite: Coconut Ladoos

TEATIME
IN
RUSSIA

Tea first came to Russia during the early seventeenth century as a gift from China to the Russian czar. Tea drinking soon became a pastime among the upper classes, and an agreement was forged between China and Russia to permit the trade of tea for furs. For well over a century, tea was brought to Russia via camel caravan, a journey that could take as long as 18 months.

As transportation sped up, tea became more affordable over time. By the nineteenth century, it was one of the country's most popular beverages, consumed after meals and throughout the day. It remains a very popular drink among Russians, and is still the traditional ending to every festive meal.

Russian tea is usually brewed in a samovar, a large, often ornately decorated urn that takes pride of place in many Russian homes. The traditional Russian method of preparing and drinking tea is distinct from all others in Europe and Asia, in that the tea is allowed to steep for a very long time. Due to the long steeping time, Indian or Chinese black tea is usually used, as this doesn't become bitter over time. In some houses, the first tea of the morning may even be made with the tea left over in the samovar from the day before. However, only a small amount of this concentrated tea is poured into individual glasses. The rest is filled up with boiling water.

Tea in Russia is usually served in glasses, rather than cups or bowls. Because glasses with hot tea are hot to the touch, they are usually placed in metal tea glass holders (see picture on opposite page). Russians tend to like their tea sweet as well as strong, and either add sugar to the glass or hold a sugar cube in their mouths as they drink. Milk is rarely added. When tea is accompanied by jam and honey, these are served in small dishes to each individual and eaten with a teaspoon in between sips of tea.

PREPARING RUSSIAN TEA

Tea prepared in a samovar often steeps for several hours, thus black Indian tea and Chinese tea are best choices, as these types will not become bitter as they steep. If you don't have a samovar, brew very strong tea in a teapot and let it steep throughout the day. To make a serving of hot tea, simply add 1 cup of hot water to 1 tablespoon of the very strong steeped tea.

PREPARATION

1. Place 2 to 3 teaspoons of loose tea leaves per cup of water into a samovar. Add boiling water and cover.

2. Let the tea steep for at least 5 minutes, or as long as all day.

3. Pour a small amount of tea into a glass and fill up with fresh boiling water. Serve with sugar, lemon slices, jam, or honey.

PECAN TEA CAKES

Rich, sweet, and indulgent, these cakes literally melt in your mouth.

INGREDIENTS

Makes 20 cakes

1 cup butter, softened

½ cup confectioners' sugar, plus more for rolling

2¼ cups all-purpose flour

1 teaspoon pure vanilla extract

¾ cup finely chopped pecans

¼ teaspoon salt

PREPARATION

1. Preheat oven to 400°F.

2. In a large bowl, cream butter with an electric mixer. Gradually add confectioners' sugar while continuing to beat. Mix until light and fluffy. Add flour, vanilla, pecans, and salt, and mix with a wooden spoon until a dough forms.

3. Break off pieces of dough, roll into 1-inch balls, and arrange 1 inch apart on a baking sheet. Bake 10 to 12 minutes, until set and golden. Transfer to a wire rack to cool just until cool enough to handle.

4. Place some confectioners' sugar in a small bowl and roll warm tea cakes in the sugar. Return coated balls to wire rack to cool completely. Roll again in confectioners' sugar before serving.

SPICED HONEY CAKE

Make this cake a couple of days in advance to allow the flavors to blend and develop.

INGREDIENTS

Makes one 8½ × 4 ½-inch cake

¾ cup honey

½ teaspoon ground cinnamon

¼ teaspoon ground nutmeg

¼ teaspoon ground cloves

1 teaspoon baking soda

¼ cup unsalted butter, softened, plus more for greasing

½ cup dark brown sugar

3 large free-range eggs, separated

2 cups all-purpose flour

¼ teaspoon salt

1 teaspoon baking powder

⅓ cup raisins

6 tablespoons dried currants

½ cup finely chopped walnuts

PREPARATION

1. Preheat oven to 350°F and grease an 8½ × 4½ × 2½-inch loaf pan with butter.

2. In a small saucepan over medium heat, bring honey to a boil, stirring constantly. Remove from heat and stir in cinnamon, nutmeg, cloves, and baking soda. Set aside to cool.

3. In a large bowl, beat together butter and brown sugar until light and fluffy. Add egg yolks one at a time, making sure each one is thoroughly incorporated before adding the next. Stir in cooled honey.

4. Sift together 1¾ cups of the flour with all of the salt and baking powder. Add gradually to butter mixture, beating constantly.

5. In a small bow, combine raisins, currants, and walnuts. Toss with remaining ¼ cup of flour until coated, then fold into batter.

6. Beat egg whites with an electric mixer until stiff peaks form. Gently fold into batter.

7. Pour batter into prepared loaf pan and place on lined baking sheet. Bake about 1½ hours, or until a toothpick inserted in the center comes out clean. Run a knife around edges of cake to loosen it from the pan, and turn out onto a wire rack. Cool completely before serving.

PLUM CAKE

Wholesome and fruity, this easy recipe is perfect for preparing when company is already on its way.

INGREDIENTS

Makes one 10-inch round cake

Cake:
¾ cup butter, plus more for greasing

1 cup sugar

1 teaspoon pure vanilla extract

4 large free-range eggs

2 cups all-purpose flour

2 teaspoons baking powder

2 pounds soft plums, halved and pitted

Topping:
1 tablespoon ground cinnamon

2 tablespoons sugar

PREPARATION

1. Preheat oven to 300°F and grease a 10-inch round cake pan with butter.

2. Prepare the cake: In a large bowl, beat butter, sugar, and vanilla with an electric mixer, until creamy. Beat in eggs one at a time. Mix in flour and baking powder.

3. Pour batter into prepared pan, even out with a spatula, and cover with plum halves. Bake about 1 hour, until golden. Check cake after 35 minutes: if already brown, cover with foil and continue baking. Let cool in pan.

4. Prepare the topping: Mix together cinnamon and sugar and sprinkle on cake before serving.

Opposite: Plum Cake

CHOCOLATE-COVERED STRAWBERRIES

Choose large, lush strawberries to maximize the elegance of this recipe.

INGREDIENTS

Makes 20 covered strawberries

20 large strawberries, with stalks and leaves

3½ ounces white chocolate, coarsely chopped

3½ ounces bittersweet chocolate, coarsely chopped

PREPARATION

1. Rinse strawberries and gently pat dry. Line a baking sheet with wax paper.

2. Melt white chocolate in the top of a double boiler, then transfer to a small bowl. Repeat with the bittersweet chocolate, making sure that the double boiler is clean so as not to lighten the bittersweet chocolate's color.

3. Holding a strawberry by the stalk, dip halfway into one of the chocolate sauces, lift out, let excess drizzle back into bowl, and lay strawberry on prepared baking sheet to harden. Repeat to cover all 20 strawberries. Refrigerate at least 15 minutes before serving to allow the chocolate to set.

BLINI

Top these small, leavened buckwheat pancakes with cream cheese and preserved cherries for a decadent snack.

INGREDIENTS

Makes 24 blini

½ cup buckwheat flour

¼ cup all-purpose flour

1½ teaspoons baking powder

1 large free-range egg, lightly beaten

¾ cup buttermilk

2 tablespoons butter, melted

½ cup crème fraîche (optional)

½ cup preserved cherries (optional)

PREPARATION

1. In a large bowl, sift together flours and baking powder. Gradually whisk in egg and buttermilk. Stir in butter.

2. Heat a large, nonstick frying pan over medium-high heat. Drop tablespoonfuls of batter into pan, a few inches apart. Cook until bubbles form on top, about 2 minutes. Flip over and cook other side until brown, about 2 minutes.

3. Transfer to a wire rack to cool. Serve with crème fraîche and preserved cherries.

WALNUT GINGER COOKIES

Crispy and nutty, these cookies are perfect for dipping into a cup of milky vanilla tea (see recipe, page 88).

INGREDIENTS

Makes 20 cookies

½ cup honey

4 tablespoons sugar

2½ cups all-purpose flour

1 tablespoon butter, softened

2 large free-range eggs, beaten

½ teaspoon baking powder

½ teaspoon ground cloves

¼ teaspoon ground ginger

1 cup chopped walnuts

PREPARATION

1. Position a rack in the middle of the oven, but do not preheat oven. Line a large baking sheet with parchment paper.

2. In a medium saucepan over medium heat, heat honey and sugar until sugar melts. Do not let honey boil. Remove from heat and mix in flour. Set aside to cool.

3. Add flour, butter, eggs, baking powder, cloves, ginger, and walnuts to honey mixture, and stir until a dough forms. Drop dough by tablespoon onto prepared baking sheet, 1 inch apart. Place sheet in oven, turn oven on to 390°F, and bake 15 to 20 minutes, until golden. Transfer to a wire rack to cool.

Opposite: Blini

TEA
COOLERS

A tall glass of iced tea on a hot day is a summertime classic. Light and refreshing, it can be made in an endless variety of flavors and sweetened according to taste. Homemade iced tea can be made using caffeinated tea, decaffeinated tea, or tisanes.

Here are a few basic tips for making homemade tea coolers:

• To prevent tea from becoming cloudy, use spring or filtered water, allow hot tea to cool at room temperature before refrigerating, and consume tea within 24 hours.

• If you want iced tea immediately, brew extra-strong tea and cool by adding cold water or ice cubes.

• Iced tea can be served sweetened or unsweetened. If sweetening with sugar or honey, add the sweetener while the tea is still warm and stir until dissolved. Use sugar syrup (see recipe, page 71) to sweeten cold tea.

SUGAR SYRUP

Serve unsweetened iced tea with a small jar of sugar syrup on the side, so that everyone can sweeten according to their individual taste.

INGREDIENTS

Makes about 1 cup

⅔ cup sugar

⅓ cup water

PREPARATION

In a small saucepan over medium heat, heat sugar and water until a syrup forms. Remove from heat and let cool.

CLASSIC ICED TEA

Break the heat with this classic summertime beverage.

INGREDIENTS

Makes about 4 cups

4 cups water

8 teaspoons loose black tea, any variety

Ice cubes

Fresh mint sprigs for garnish

Lemon slices for garnish

Sugar syrup (optional; see recipe, this page)

PREPARATION

1. In a medium saucepan, bring water to a boil, remove from heat, add tea leaves, and cover. Let steep 3 to 5 minutes.

2. Pour tea through a strainer into a heatproof pitcher. Let cool to room temperature, then refrigerate until chilled.

3. To serve, pour over ice cubes into a glass and garnish with mint and lemon. Serve with sugar syrup on the side, if desired.

SWEET SOUTHERN ICED TEA

The Southern states are famous for their sweet iced tea. Add white sugar or another sweetener to the hot water or tea before chilling.

INGREDIENTS

Makes about 8 cups

3 cups water

3 teaspoons loose black tea

½ to ¾ cup sugar

5 cups cold water

Ice cubes

PREPARATION

1. In a medium saucepan, bring water to a boil, remove from heat, add tea leaves, and cover. Let steep 3 to 5 minutes.

2. Pour tea through a strainer into a heatproof pitcher. Add sugar and mix until dissolved. Add cold water and refrigerate until chilled.

3. To serve, pour over ice cubes into a glass.

ICED JASMINE TEA

Using sparkling water makes this tea light and bubbly.

INGREDIENTS

Makes about 6 cups

1 cup packed brown sugar

4 cups water

3 tablespoons loose jasmine tea

1¼ cups sparkling water

Ice cubes

Fresh mint sprigs for garnish

Lemon slices for garnish

PREPARATION

1. In a small saucepan over low heat, heat sugar and 1 cup water until a syrup forms. Remove from heat and set aside.

2. In a separate saucepan, bring remaining water to a boil, remove from heat, add tea leaves, and cover. Let steep 8 minutes.

3. Pour tea through a strainer into a heatproof pitcher. Stir in brown sugar syrup. Let cool to room temperature.

4. Stir in sparkling water. Refrigerate until chilled.

5. To serve, pour over ice cubes into a glass and garnish with mint sprigs and lemon slices.

ICED SPICE TEA

Diverse spices in this drink make it positively invigorating!

INGREDIENTS

Makes about 7 cups

1 teaspoon whole cloves

1 cinnamon stick

6 cups water

4 teaspoons loose black tea

½ cup sugar

¾ cup freshly squeezed orange juice

1 tablespoon freshly squeezed lemon juice

Ice cubes

PREPARATION

1. In a large saucepan over high heat, bring cloves, cinnamon stick, and water to a boil. Remove from heat, add tea leaves, and cover. Let steep 3 to 5 minutes.

2. In a small saucepan over low heat, combine sugar and juices and simmer about 5 minutes, until sugar dissolves.

3. Pour tea through a fine mesh strainer into a heatproof pitcher. Stir in juice mixture. Let cool to room temperature, then refrigerate until chilled.

4. To serve, pour over ice cubes.

Opposite: Iced Jasmine Tea

SUN TEA

This slow-steep tea is perfect for making on lazy summer days.

INGREDIENTS

Makes about 8 cups

4 teaspoons loose black tea

8 cups water

Ice cubes

Sugar syrup (optional; see recipe, page 71)

Freshly squeezed lemon juice (optional)

PREPARATION

1. Place tea leaves in a transparent pitcher with tight-fitting lid. Pour in water, cover, and place outdoors in full sun. Let steep 2 to 3 hours.

2. Pour tea through a strainer into another pitcher. Refrigerate until chilled.

3. To serve, pour over ice cubes into a glass. Serve with sugar syrup and lemon juice on the side, if desired.

MINT TEA PUNCH

With a refreshing combination of fresh juices and mint, this tea is lovely for serving at brunch.

INGREDIENTS

Makes about 9 cups

3 cups water

12 fresh mint sprigs

4 tea bags black tea

1 cup sugar

1 cup freshly squeezed orange juice

¼ cup freshly squeezed lemon juice

5 cups cold water

Ice cubes

Citrus slices for garnish

Mint leaves for garnish

PREPARATION

1. In a medium saucepan, bring water to a boil. Remove from heat and add mint and tea bags. Cover and let steep 4 minutes. Remove tea bags, squeezing excess liquid back into saucepan. Allow mint to steep another 4 minutes, then remove.

2. Add sugar and mix until dissolved. Transfer to a heatproof pitcher and stir in juices and cold water. Refrigerate until chilled.

3. To serve, pour over ice cubes into a glass and garnish with citrus slices and mint leaves.

CRANBERRY ICED TEA COOLER

The spicy sweetness of the ginger ale combines perfectly with the tanginess of the cranberry juice.

INGREDIENTS

Makes about 12 cups

5 cups water

5 teaspoons loose black tea

1 cinnamon stick

1½ cups cranberry-apple juice

1½ cups freshly squeezed orange juice

3 tablespoons freshly squeezed lemon juice

5 teaspoons sugar

4 cups ginger ale

Ice cubes

Orange slices for garnish

PREPARATION

1. In a large saucepan, bring water to a boil, add tea leaves and cinnamon stick, remove from heat, and cover. Let steep 3 to 5 minutes.

2. Pour tea through a strainer into a heatproof pitcher. Add juices and sugar and mix well.

3. Stir in ginger ale. Refrigerate until chilled.

4. To serve, pour over ice cubes into a glass and garnish with orange slices.

ICED HONEY, LIME, AND GINGER TEA

Soothing and refreshing, this tea is a little tangy, too.

INGREDIENTS

Makes about 4 cups

1 stalk lemongrass

4 cups water

4 teaspoons loose green tea

2 teaspoons grated fresh ginger

½ cup honey

2 tablespoons freshly squeezed lime juice

Ice cubes

Lemon and lime slices for garnish

Fresh lemon verbena sprigs for garnish

PREPARATION

1. Bruise lemongrass by pressing it with the back of a spoon.

2. In a medium saucepan, bring water to a boil. Remove from heat and let cool slightly. Add lemongrass, tea leaves, and ginger. Cover and let steep 3 to 5 minutes.

3. Pour tea through a fine mesh strainer into a heatproof pitcher. Mix in honey and lime juice. Let cool to room temperature, then refrigerate until chilled.

4. To serve, pour over ice and citrus slices into a glass and garnish with lemon verbena.

ICED SENCHA TEA

Fans of green tea will be delighted with this chilled alternative.

INGREDIENTS

Makes about 1½ cups

1½ tablespoons loose sencha tea leaves

Ice cubes, plus more for serving

Fresh mint sprigs for garnish

Lemon slice for garnish

PREPARATION

1. Place tea leaves into an individual-size teapot and fill with ice cubes. Let sit at room temperature until ice melts.

2. Pour tea through a fine mesh strainer into a glass. Add ice and garnish with mint and lemon.

ICED APPLE AND SPICE TEA

The scent from this tea is wonderfully spicy.

INGREDIENTS

Makes about 6 cups

3 cups apple juice

⅓ cup honey

¼ teaspoon ground cinnamon

¼ teaspoon ground ginger

¼ teaspoon ground nutmeg

¼ teaspoon ground cloves

3 cups water

6 teaspoons loose black tea

Ice cubes

Lemon slices for garnish

Apple slices for garnish

PREPARATION

1. In a medium saucepan over medium heat, mix together the apple juice, honey, cinnamon, ginger, nutmeg, and cloves. Heat about 5 minutes, stirring occasionally, until mixture thickens. Remove from heat and set aside.

2. In a separate saucepan, bring water to a boil, add tea leaves, remove from heat, and cover. Let steep 3 to 5 minutes.

3. Pour tea through a fine mesh strainer into a heatproof pitcher. Add apple juice mixture. Let cool to room temperature, then refrigerate until chilled.

4. To serve, pour over ice cubes into a glass and garnish with lemon and apple slices.

Opposite: Iced Sencha Tea

THAI ICED TEA

Orange blossom water gives this beverage its distinct floral aroma. It can be found in health food stores and Middle Eastern specialty shops.

INGREDIENTS

Serves 2

4 cups water

2 star anise

½ vanilla bean or
¼ teaspoon pure vanilla extract

6 whole cloves

½ cinnamon stick

1 teaspoon grated fresh ginger

2 teaspoons loose black tea

½ cup sugar

2 teaspoons orange blossom water

½ cup coconut cream

2 star anise for garnish

PREPARATION

1. In a large saucepan over high heat, bring water, anise, vanilla, cloves, cinnamon, ginger, and tea to a boil. Continue boiling about 3 minutes, then remove from heat. Pour tea through a fine mesh strainer into a heatproof pitcher. Add sugar and stir until dissolved. Let cool to room temperature.

2. Stir in orange blossom water and refrigerate until ready to serve.

3. To serve, pour through a fine mesh strainer into two glasses. Top each glass with ¼ cup coconut cream and garnish with star anise. Serve immediately, without stirring.

Opposite: Thai Iced Tea

ICED CHAMOMILE, LEMON, AND LAVENDER TEA

This pretty tea has a calming effect.

INGREDIENTS

Serves 2

4 cups water

2 teaspoons dried chamomile flowers

2 teaspoons dried lavender flowers

4 teaspoons honey

2 teaspoons freshly squeezed lemon juice

Fresh mint sprigs for garnish

Lemon slices for garnish

PREPARATION

1. In a medium saucepan, bring water to a boil, remove from heat, add flowers, and cover. Let steep 20 minutes.

2. Pour liquid through a fine mesh strainer into a heatproof pitcher. Stir in honey and lemon juice. Let cool to room temperature, then refrigerate until chilled.

3. To serve, pour over ice cubes into a glass and garnish with mint sprigs and lemon slices.

Flavored Frozen Tea Cubes

These colorful, delicately flavored ice cubes can be used instead of regular ice cubes to chill and add flavor to water, sparkling water, and fruit juices.

Opposite: Flavored Frozen Tea Cubes

LEMON LIME TEA CUBES

INGREDIENTS

Makes about 16 ice cubes

2 cups water

2 teaspoons loose black tea

1 tablespoon sugar

1 tablespoon freshly squeezed lemon juice

1 tablespoon freshly squeezed lime juice

1 tablespoon lemon zest, diced

1 tablespoon lime zest, diced

PREPARATION

1. In a small saucepan, bring water to a boil, add tea leaves, remove from heat, and cover. Let steep 3 to 5 minutes.

2. Pour tea through a fine mesh strainer into a heatproof pitcher. Mix in sugar. Let cool to room temperature.

3. Mix in juices and zest. Transfer to an ice cube tray and freeze.

GINGER AND HONEY TEA CUBES

INGREDIENTS

Makes about 16 ice cubes

2 cups water

2 teaspoons loose black tea

1 tablespoon honey

1 tablespoon grated fresh ginger

1 tablespoon lemon zest, diced

PREPARATION

1. In a small saucepan, bring water to a boil, add tea leaves, remove from heat, and cover. Let steep 3 to 5 minutes.

2. Pour tea through a fine mesh strainer into a heatproof pitcher. Mix in honey. Let cool to room temperature.

3. Squeeze ginger in a garlic press to release the juices. Discard ginger flesh and mix juice into tea. Stir in lemon zest. Transfer to an ice cube tray and freeze.

TEA
COMFORTERS

Is there any better way to warm up on a cold winter day than with a nice hot cup of tea? Thank goodness there are so many delicious ways of preparing it! Rich, milky, spicy, or sweet, hot tea beverages are perfect for warming up after a brisk snowy walk, or for just sitting on the porch and watching the snow fall. Of course, hot tea can also be consumed when the weather isn't cold. It's lovely served after a meal, during a midday break, or in the evening when you want to unwind after a busy day.

CHOCOLATE CHAI

When you can't decide whether you want tea or hot chocolate, resolve the issue with this combination of both!

INGREDIENTS

Makes about 2¼ cups

¼ cup water

1 teaspoon loose black tea

3 tablespoons sugar

2 tablespoons pure cocoa powder

2 cups whole milk

1 teaspoon pure vanilla extract

½ teaspoon ground cinnamon

½ teaspoon ground nutmeg

Sweetened whipped cream for garnish

2 cinnamon sticks for garnish

PREPARATION

1. In a small saucepan, bring water to a boil, add tea leaves, remove from heat, and cover. Let steep 3 to 5 minutes.

2. Pour tea through a fine mesh strainer into another saucepan over high heat. Stir in sugar and cocoa and return to a boil. Reduce heat, and mix in milk, vanilla, cinnamon, and nutmeg. Continue to heat about 8 minutes, until it thickens.

3. Pour into mugs, garnish with whipped cream and cinnamon sticks, and serve immediately.

VERY SPICY CHAI

This fragrant tea will fill your kitchen with the rich scents of cardamom, licorice, and fennel.

INGREDIENTS

Makes about 9 cups

7 cups water

1 tablespoon fennel seeds

1 tablespoon cardamom pods

6 whole cloves

6 whole black peppercorns

1 tablespoon dried licorice root, chopped

1 tablespoon grated fresh ginger

1 cinnamon stick

2 star anise

2 teaspoons loose black tea

4 tablespoons brown sugar

2 cups whole milk

PREPARATION

1. In a large saucepan over high heat, bring water and spices to a boil, then reduce heat to low and simmer 20 minutes.

2. Add tea leaves, remove from heat, and cover. Let steep 3 to 5 minutes. Mix in sugar and milk, stirring until sugar is dissolved.

3. Pour tea through a fine mesh strainer into mugs and serve immediately.

TEA NOG

Celebrate the season with this traditional drink. Perfect for sipping while baking holiday cookies or wrapping presents.

INGREDIENTS

Makes about 4 cups

1 cup water

6 teaspoons loose black tea

2 large free-range eggs, beaten

One 14-ounce can condensed milk

4 cups whole milk

1 teaspoon pure vanilla extract

¼ teaspoon salt

Sweetened whipped cream for garnish

Ground nutmeg for garnish

PREPARATION

1. In a small saucepan, bring water to a boil, add tea leaves, remove from heat, and cover. Let steep 5 minutes.

2. Pour tea through a fine mesh strainer into another saucepan over medium heat. Whisk in eggs, milks, vanilla, and salt. Continue to heat for about 5 minutes, whisking constantly, until mixture thickens.

3. Pour into mugs, garnish with whipped cream and nutmeg, and serve immediately.

KASHMIRI CHAI

This chai is made with green tea and often brewed in a samovar. Powdered almonds give it a distinct thickness.

INGREDIENTS

Makes about 5½ cups

5½ cups cold water

5 teaspoons sugar, or more to taste

½ teaspoon ground cinnamon

½ teaspoon ground cardamom

6 strands saffron

2 teaspoons loose green tea

1 to 2 tablespoons powdered almonds

PREPARATION

1. In a medium saucepan over high heat, bring water, sugar, cinnamon, cardamom, and saffron to a boil. Boil 5 to 10 minutes, until water turns deep brown and becomes fragrant.

2. Add tea leaves, remove from heat, and cover. Let steep 3 to 5 minutes.

3. Pour tea through a fine mesh strainer into mugs. Mix ¼ to ½ teaspoon powdered almonds into each cup and serve immediately.

Opposite: Tea Nog

HOT CIDER TEA

Warm and comforting on a chilly winter evening.

INGREDIENTS

Makes about 4 cups

2 cups apple cider

2 cups water

8 whole cloves

5 allspice berries

1 cinnamon stick, plus more for garnish

½ orange, sliced

2 tablespoons honey

2 teaspoons loose black tea

PREPARATION

1. In a medium heavy saucepan over low heat, warm apple cider, water, cloves, allspice, cinnamon stick, orange slices, and honey for 10 to 15 minutes, until fragrant.

2. Add tea leaves and continue heating another 4 minutes.

3. Pour liquid through a fine mesh strainer into mugs, garnish each mug with a cinnamon stick, and serve immediately.

MILKY VANILLA TEA

Few things are as comforting as a mug of warm milky tea. This version is enhanced with vanilla and light brown sugar.

INGREDIENTS

Makes about 2½ cups

2 cups whole milk

½ cup light cream

2 teaspoons light brown sugar

1 vanilla bean, or 1 teaspoon pure vanilla extract

2 teaspoons loose black tea

Ground cinnamon for garnish

PREPARATION

1. In a medium heavy saucepan over medium heat, bring milk to scalding point. Reduce heat to low and stir in cream, brown sugar, vanilla, and tea. Let simmer 3 to 5 minutes.

2. Pour liquid through a fine mesh strainer into mugs, sprinkle with cinnamon to garnish, and serve immediately.

Opposite: Hot Cider Tea

SPICY CRANBERRY TEA

This tea is a fragrant way to banish winter chills.

INGREDIENTS

Makes about 4 cups

1 cup apple juice

1 cup freshly squeezed orange juice

1 cup cranberry juice

2 teaspoons freshly squeezed lemon juice

1 cup water

4 teaspoons light brown sugar

4 teaspoons loose black tea

1 cinnamon stick

8 whole cloves

Lemon slices for garnish

2 star anise for garnish

2 tablespoons sliced fresh ginger for garnish

PREPARATION

1. In a medium heavy saucepan over high heat, bring juices, water, and sugar to a boil. Reduce heat to medium and add the tea, cinnamon stick, and cloves. Let simmer about 5 minutes, until fragrant.

2. Pour liquid through a fine mesh strainer into mugs, garnish with lemon slices, star anise, and ginger, and serve immediately.

CHAI LATTE

This tea is a little milkier than regular chai, making it just a bit more indulgent.

INGREDIENTS

Makes about 4 cups

2 cups whole milk

2 cups water

6 cardamom pods

1 teaspoon grated fresh ginger

6 whole cloves

2 cinnamon sticks

2 whole black peppercorns

2 whole nutmeg, or ½ teaspoon ground nutmeg

4 teaspoons honey

2 teaspoons light brown sugar

4 teaspoons loose black tea

Ground cinnamon for garnish

PREPARATION

1. In a medium saucepan over medium heat, warm milk and water.

2. Bruise cardamom pods by pressing them with the back of a spoon. Add to saucepan with ginger, cloves, cinnamon, peppercorns, nutmeg, honey, brown sugar, and tea, and increase heat to high. When liquid boils, reduce heat to medium and continue cooking, stirring occasionally, until the tea deepens in color and becomes very fragrant.

3. Pour tea through a fine mesh strainer into mugs, garnish with ground cinnamon, and serve immediately.

Opposite: Spicy Cranberry Tea

Cardamon

Peppermint

Ginger

Rosehip

Star anise

Chamomile

Lavender

Lemongrass

Cinnamon

Rosemary

TISANES

Tisanes—also known as infusions or herbal teas—can be made from a wide variety of fresh or dried plants. They are prepared by pouring boiling or very hot water over leaves, flowers, bark, seeds, or roots, steeping for several minutes, then pouring through a strainer. Fancy gadgets can be used to make tisanes, but all you really need is a pot or kettle for heating water, a teapot or other heatproof vessel for steeping, and a fine mesh strainer.

Bark, seeds, and roots must be decocted first in order to release their flavor. To decoct roots or bark, cut them into very small pieces. To decoct seeds, crush them with a mortar and pestle or with the back of a spoon.

Tisanes made with spices, such as cloves, ginger, or cinnamon, generally have a strong flavor; those made with flowers, such as chamomile and jasmine, have a delicate flavor. Strengthen or weaken the flavor of your tisane according to your taste by adjusting the amount of spice or flower you use. Most tisanes are delicate enough to drink without sweetening, but many people like to add sugar or honey; milk is rarely added. Tisanes can be consumed warm or cold, but cold tisanes should be brewed extra strong so that the flavor isn't diminished when ice is added.

CITRUS BLEND

Citrus is a common flowering plant native to tropical and subtropical southeast Asia. The flowers are strongly scented and the fruits are rich in flavonoids, citric acid, and vitamin C. Citrus fruits are commonly consumed to boost the immune system, and to alleviate the symptoms of colds and flu. The pulp, peels, zest, and juice from these fruits are used to flavor and garnish teas, as well as other drinks and culinary dishes.

INGREDIENTS

Makes about 6 teaspoons

2 different citrus fruits (orange, lemon, lime, or tangerine)

4 tablespoons loose black tea

PREPARATION

1. Preheat oven to 250°F. Line a baking sheet with parchment paper.

2. Scrub fruit and dry with a clean cloth. Remove zest in strips using a vegetable peeler. Try to remove the colored part only, as the white part is very bitter. Cut zest into small pieces and scatter on prepared baking sheet. Bake 20 minutes. Let cool.

3. Combine tea leaves and zest in an airtight container and store until ready to use.

4. To prepare a cup of tea, place 1 teaspoon Citrus Blend in a teapot and pour in 1 cup boiling water. Let steep 5 to 8 minutes. Pour through a fine mesh strainer into a cup and serve.

LINDEN FLOWERS

These delicate yellow flowers are native to northern Europe, Asia, and northern America. Though the flower is sometimes referred to as lime blossom, it is not related to the citrus fruit. Linden flower tisane is said to aid digestion and to be an effective remedy for common colds and flu.

INGREDIENTS

Makes 2 cups

2 cups water

2 to 3 teaspoons dried linden flowers, or 3 teaspoons fresh linden flowers

PREPARATION

In a small saucepan, heat water until small bubbles begin to rise from the bottom of the pan, but do not boil. Remove from heat, add linden flowers, and cover. Let steep 10 to 15 minutes. Pour through a fine mesh strainer into a mug and serve.

CHAMOMILE

This is an annual plant of the
sunflower family. The flowers have
white petals and a yellow center.
Chamomile is one of the most
popular types of tisanes, often taken
for its gentle sedative properties.

INGREDIENTS

Makes 2 cups

2 cups water

2 teaspoons dried chamomile
flowers

PREPARATION

In a small saucepan, bring water
to a boil, remove from heat, add
chamomile, and cover. Let steep
10 to 15 minutes. Pour through
a fine mesh strainer into a cup
and serve.

Opposite: Chamomile

ELDERFLOWER

These are white, fluffy flowers
native to Europe. Tisanes made
from them have a golden color and
a malted honey aroma. The plant
is said to be good for boosting the
immune system, and is well-suited
for relaxing in the evening.

INGREDIENTS

Makes 2 cups

2 cups water

2 teaspoons dried elderflowers

PREPARATION

In a small saucepan, bring water
to a boil, remove from heat, add
elderflowers, and cover. Let steep
10 to 15 minutes. Pour through
a fine mesh strainer into a cup
and serve.

FENNEL

Fennel is native to the
Mediterranean and southwestern
Asia. It is similar both in flavor
and appearance to anise. Many
believe it to be good for digestion.
In some cultures, cooled fennel tea is
even given to infants to treat colic.

INGREDIENTS

Makes 2 cups

2 cups water

1 teaspoon dried fennel seeds

PREPARATION

1. Crush fennel seeds with a
mortar and pestle or with the
back of a spoon.

2. In a small saucepan, bring
water to a boil, remove from
heat, add fennel, and cover.
Let steep 10 minutes.

3. Pour through a fine mesh
strainer into a cup and serve.

ROOIBOS

This South African plant is also known as Red Bush or South African Red Tea. Its flowers are yellow, but the infusion brewed from its leaves is red. Rooibos tisane is naturally caffeine-free and rich in antioxidants.

INGREDIENTS

Makes 2 cups

2 cups water

2 teaspoons dried rooibos leaves

PREPARATION

In a small saucepan, bring water to a boil, remove from heat, add rooibos, and cover. Let steep 2 to 5 minutes. Pour through a fine mesh strainer into a cup and serve.

PEPPERMINT

Native to Europe, this plant is actually a hybrid of watermint and spearmint. Its extreme minty-ness is used to flavor diverse items, including ice cream, chewing gum, and toothpaste. Peppermint tisane is said to be an effective remedy for upset stomachs and tight muscles.

INGREDIENTS

Makes 2 cups

2 cups water

2 teaspoons dry peppermint leaves

PREPARATION

In a small saucepan, bring water to a boil, remove from heat, add peppermint, and cover. Let steep 10 to 15 minutes. Pour through a fine mesh strainer into a cup and serve.

GINGER

Ginger is originally native to China. It has a pungent taste that is enjoyed in many forms as a spice: fresh, powdered, pickled, and even as juice and paste. Ginger tisane is believed to improve blood circulation and digestion, and to reduce nausea.

INGREDIENTS

Makes 2 cups

2 cups water

1-inch piece fresh ginger, thinly sliced

PREPARATION

In a small saucepan, bring water to a boil, remove from heat, add ginger, and cover. Let steep 15 to 20 minutes. Pour through a fine mesh strainer into a cup and serve.

Opposite: Rooibos

COOKING
WITH TEA

Substituting tea or tisane for the usual cooking liquids can add interesting flavor and distinctive color to otherwise ordinary dishes. Teas and tisanes can be used to flavor grains, fish, poultry, meat, cakes, or desserts. Try the recipes on the following pages to get a taste of the possibilities, then experiment with some of your own favorite recipes. Remember that 1 teaspoon loose tea leaves can be substituted for 1 tea bag, and vice versa, so feel free to adapt the recipe according to your preference. See Common Substitutions, page 13.

TEA-SMOKED SALMON

This Chinese technique gives salmon a distinct smoked flavor. Open the windows in your kitchen while preparing as the method generates lots of smoke.

INGREDIENTS

Serves 4

½ cup brown sugar

½ cup long grain rice

½ cup loose black tea

Four 5-ounce salmon fillets, with skin

Olive oil

Salt and freshly ground black pepper

PREPARATION

1. Line a deep roasting pan with aluminum foil.

2. In a medium bowl, mix together sugar, rice, and tea leaves. Press mixture into bottom of prepared pan and cover with another piece of foil. Place on stove over low heat.

3. When mixture begins to smoke, arrange salmon on foil skin side up. Drizzle with olive oil and season with salt and pepper to taste. Cover pan with a tight-fitting lid, or seal well with foil. Cook over low heat for 15 minutes. (Expect quite a lot of smoke!)

4. Remove from heat and wait for smoke to dissipate before removing cover. Serve immediately.

TEA-SMOKED CHICKEN

This technique is quite smoky, so open the windows and turn on a fan or vent, if possible.

INGREDIENTS

Serves 2

¾ cup packed brown sugar

¾ cup long grain rice

¾ cup loose jasmine tea

2 boneless chicken breasts

1 teaspoon sesame or peanut oil

Salt

PREPARATION

1. Line a deep roasting pan with aluminum foil.

2. In a medium bowl, mix together sugar, rice, and tea leaves. Press mixture into bottom of prepared pan and cover with another piece of foil. Place on stove over low heat.

3. Rub chicken with sesame oil, sprinkle with salt, and place on a wire rack. When tea mixture begins to smoke, set rack in roasting pan and cover pan with a tight-fitting lid, or seal well with foil. Increase heat to high and cook for 15 minutes. (Expect quite a lot of smoke!)

4. Remove from heat and wait for smoke to dissipate before removing cover. Serve immediately.

ROOIBOS COUSCOUS WITH SNOW PEAS AND SHITAKE MUSHROOMS

This dish has a distinct reddish color and sweet woody flavor.

INGREDIENTS

Serves 4

1 cup water

1 rooibos tea bag

1 cup medium couscous

½ teaspoon vegetable or chicken soup powder

¼ teaspoon vegetable oil

2 tablespoons toasted sesame oil

1 tablespoon soy sauce

1 teaspoon butter

½ pound shitake mushrooms, sliced

1 teaspoon grated fresh ginger

1 scallion, finely sliced

1 cup fresh snow peas

Salt and freshly ground black pepper

1 small red chili, shredded, for garnish

1 tablespoon finely chopped fresh basil for garnish

PREPARATION

1. In a small saucepan, bring water to a boil, add tea bag, cover, and remove from heat. Let steep 3 to 5 minutes. Remove tea bag, squeezing excess liquid back into saucepan.

2. In a heatproof bowl, combine couscous, soup powder, and vegetable oil. Pour in tea but do not stir. Cover and let stand 10 minutes. Fluff with a fork.

3. In a medium saucepan over medium heat, heat sesame oil, soy sauce, and butter. When butter is melted, add mushrooms, ginger, and scallion. Reduce heat to medium-low and cook about 3 minutes. Add snow peas and cook another minute.

4. Stir vegetables into couscous and season with salt and pepper to taste. Garnish with red chili and basil. Serve warm.

WHITE FISH IN PEPPERMINT AND LEMON TEA

The delicate flavors in this dish make it a perfect summertime meal.

INGREDIENTS

Serves 4

1 cup water

4 peppermint tea bags

Four 5-ounce fillets white fish

2 tablespoons freshly squeezed lemon juice

1 large lemon, sliced into rounds

Coarse sea salt

1 teaspoon honey

1 tablespoon olive oil

12 spears (¾ pound) cooked asparagus

Lemon slices for garnish

PREPARATION

1. Preheat oven to 450°F.

2. In a small saucepan, bring water to a boil, add tea bags, cover, and remove from heat. Let steep 7 minutes. Remove tea bags, squeezing excess liquid back into saucepan.

3. Add lemon juice to tea and pour over fish. Arrange lemon slices on each fillet, sprinkle with coarse salt, and drizzle with honey and olive oil. Cover with aluminum foil and bake 18 to 20 minutes, until fish is cooked through.

4. Lay several asparagus spears on each plate, top with a fish fillet, and garnish with lemon slices.

Opposite: White Fish in Peppermint and Lemon Tea

PEPPERMINT LAMB CHOPS

The combination of mint and lamb is classic in Mediterranean cooking.

INGREDIENTS

Serves 2

1 cup water

1 peppermint tea bag

4 tablespoons freshly squeezed lemon juice

Two 8-ounce lamb chops

1 tablespoon olive oil

1 small onion, thinly sliced

8 small Portobello or button mushrooms

1 teaspoon brown sugar

Salt and freshly ground black pepper

PREPARATION

1. In a small saucepan, bring water to a boil, add tea bag, cover, and remove from heat. Let steep 5 minutes.

2. Remove tea bag, squeezing excess liquid back into saucepan. Set aside 1 tablespoon tea and mix remainder with lemon juice.

3. Place lamb chops in a shallow dish and pour over tea-lemon mixture. Cover and marinate, refrigerated, at least 2 hours.

4. Heat olive oil in a frying pan over high heat. Sear lamb chops for 2 to 3 minutes on each side, then reduce heat to medium and sauté about 10 minutes on each side. Transfer cooked lamb chops to serving plates.

5. Add onions and mushrooms to pan (along with more oil if necessary) and sauté about 3 to 5 minutes, until soft. Stir in sugar and remaining tablespoon tea, and season with salt and pepper. Pour over lamb chops and serve immediately.

CREAMY POTATO CHAMOMILE SOUP

Warm, comforting, and fragrant, this soup will drive away any winter blues.

INGREDIENTS

Serves 4 to 6

1 tablespoon butter

1 tablespoon olive oil

1 leek, finely chopped

1 celery stalk, finely sliced

Salt and freshly ground black pepper

3 cups water

4 chamomile tea bags

1 tablespoon vegetable or chicken soup powder

8 small potatoes, peeled and cut into large chunks

1 bay leaf

2 fresh sage leaves

½ cup heavy cream

¼ teaspoon nutmeg

PREPARATION

1. In a medium saucepan over low heat, heat butter and oil until butter is melted. Add leek, celery, and salt to taste. Cook over low heat until vegetables are tender, about 3 to 5 minutes. Set aside.

2. In a large stockpot, bring 2 cups of the water to a boil, add tea bags, and cover. Let steep 7 minutes. Remove tea bags, squeezing excess liquid back into pot.

3. Return tea to stove and bring to a boil over high heat. Add cooked vegetables, remaining cup water, soup powder, potatoes, bay leaf, and sage leaves. Reduce heat to medium, cover, and simmer about 25 minutes, until potatoes are soft.

4. Remove bay and sage leaves and insert an immersion blender into pot. (Alternatively, transfer soup to a standing blender.) Purée until smooth. Stir in cream, nutmeg, and salt and pepper to taste. Transfer to bowls and serve immediately.

MARBLED TEA EGGS

These eggs add a striking effect to any meal. Cut in half or quarters and serve with a bowl of salad greens.

INGREDIENTS

Makes 12 eggs

12 large hard-boiled eggs, cooled

2 tablespoons loose black tea

2 cinnamon sticks

3 to 4 star anise

2 tablespoons soy sauce

1 tablespoon salt

¼ tablespoon sugar

Water

PREPARATION

1. Crack egg shells all over by tapping with the back of a heavy spoon, but do not remove shells.

2. Place eggs, tea, cinnamon, star anise, soy sauce, salt, and sugar in a large saucepan, and add water to cover. Over medium heat, boil 2 to 2 ½ hours, checking every 30 minutes and adding water as necessary to ensure that eggs remain immersed in liquid.

3. Remove eggs to a plate covered with paper towels and let cool to room temperature. Peel and serve.

CHAMOMILE-INFUSED WHITE CHOCOLATE SAUCE

Served warm, this sauce can be drizzled over fruit tarts, strawberry shortcakes, and hot puddings. Serve chilled, it can be spread on cookies and cakes.

INGREDIENTS

Makes about 1 cup

⅔ cup heavy cream

2 chamomile tea bags

7 ounces white chocolate, coarsely chopped

2 tablespoons butter

¼ teaspoon pure vanilla extract

PREPARATION

1. In a small saucepan over medium heat, bring cream just to scalding point. Remove from heat, add tea bags, and cover. Let steep 30 minutes. Remove tea bags, squeezing excess liquid back into saucepan.

2. Melt chocolate and butter in the top of a double boiler. Whisk in infused cream and vanilla. Serve warm, or chill until it thickens, and spread on baked goods.

Opposite: Marbled Tea Eggs

LAVENDER SHORTBREAD COOKIES

*These cookies are fragrant and elegant. Use flower-shaped cutters to make them
particularly pretty.*

INGREDIENTS

Makes 36 cookies

2 cups unsalted butter, softened

1½ cups sifted confectioners' sugar, plus more for sprinkling

1½ teaspoons pure vanilla extract

4 cups sifted all-purpose flour, plus more for dusting

¾ teaspoon salt

2 tablespoons dried lavender flowers, plus more for sprinkling

1 tablespoon grated lemon zest

PREPARATION

1. In a large bowl, beat butter and sugar with an electric mixer, until fluffy. Add vanilla, flour, and salt and beat at low speed until well combined. Stir in lavender and lemon zest.

2. On a lightly floured surface, divide dough into four equal parts. Roll each part into a ball and flatten into a disk. Cover with plastic wrap and refrigerate at least 30 minutes.

3. Remove dough from refrigerator and let sit 10 to 15 minutes at room temperature.

4. Preheat oven to 300°F and position rack in center of oven. Line two large baking sheets with parchment paper.

5. On a lightly floured surface, unwrap dough and roll out with a floured rolling pin until ¼ inch thick. Cut out cookies with a 1-inch round cookie cutter dipped in flour to prevent sticking.

6. Arrange cookies on prepared baking sheets, sprinkle with confectioners' sugar, and press in the lavender. Bake 15 to 20 minutes, until edges are golden brown. Let cool completely before removing from pan.

JASMINE AND CITRUS POUND CAKE

Enhance a standard pound cake with the subtle flavors of jasmine and citrus.

INGREDIENTS

Makes one 8-inch round cake

Cake:

½ cup whole milk

1 teaspoon loose jasmine tea

4 large free-range eggs

1¾ cups sugar

½ teaspoon salt

¼ cup cream

2 teaspoons grated lemon zest

2 teaspoons grated orange zest

2¾ cups all-purpose flour

1¼ teaspoons baking powder

½ cup butter, melted

¼ cup freshly squeezed orange juice

Frosting:

½ cup heavy cream

2 teaspoons loose jasmine tea

3½ ounces white chocolate, melted

1½ cups confectioners' sugar

1 tablespoon grated orange zest

Fresh jasmine flowers for garnish

PREPARATION

1. Preheat oven to 325°F and line an 8-inch round cake pan with parchment paper.

2. Prepare the cake: In a small saucepan over medium heat, bring milk just to scalding point. Remove from heat, add tea leaves, and cover. Let steep 8 minutes. Pour infused milk through a fine mesh strainer into a heatproof bowl and set aside.

3. In a large bowl, beat eggs with an electric mixer until fluffy. Gradually beat in sugar and salt. Stir in infused milk, cream, and zests.

4. In a separate bowl, sift together flour and baking powder. Gradually add to egg mixture, mixing on low speed until smooth. Blend in butter.

5. Pour batter into prepared pan and bake 60 to 75 minutes, until a toothpick inserted in the center comes out clean. Let cool slightly in pan.

6. Prick around top of cake with a toothpick and brush with orange juice. Let cake cool completely in pan, then transfer to a serving dish.

7. Prepare the frosting: In a small saucepan over medium heat, bring cream just to scalding point. Remove from heat, add tea leaves, and cover. Let steep 8 minutes.

8. Pour infused cream through a fine mesh strainer into a heatproof bowl. Whisk in white chocolate, confectioners' sugar, and orange zest. Cover with plastic wrap and chill at least 15 minutes.

9. Spread frosting on cake with a spatula and garnish with fresh jasmine flowers.

GREEN TEA ICE CREAM

With its bright green color, this dessert will naturally attract people with curious taste buds.

INGREDIENTS

Makes about 4 cups

1½ cups whole milk

4 tea bags green tea

8 large free-range egg yolks

1 cup sugar

1 teaspoon salt

2½ cups heavy cream

1 teaspoon pure vanilla extract

PREPARATION

1. In a small saucepan over medium heat, bring milk just to scalding point. Remove from heat, add tea bags, and cover. Let steep 3 to 5 minutes.

2. Remove tea bags, squeezing excess liquid back into saucepan. Return infused milk to medium heat and whisk in egg yolks, sugar, salt, cream, and vanilla extract. Continue to stir while heating for about 5 minutes, until thickened. Transfer to a heatproof and freezer-safe container and let cool to room temperature, then freeze 3 to 4 hours, until ice cream has set.

LAVENDER WHIPPED CREAM

This delicately flavored cream is lovely with scones, fresh berries, and fresh fruit tarts.

INGREDIENTS

Makes 1 cup

1 heaping tablespoon dried lavender flowers

2 heaping tablespoons sugar

1 cup heavy whipping cream

1 teaspoon pure vanilla extract

PREPARATION

1. Crush lavender using a mortar and pestle.

2. In a small bowl, combine lavender, sugar, and cream. Cover and refrigerate 1 hour.

3. Pour infused cream through a fine mesh strainer into a large bowl. Add vanilla and whip with an electric mixer until stiff, about 2 to 3 minutes. Serve immediately or refrigerate until ready to serve.

Opposite: Green Tea Ice Cream

Hosting
a Tea Party

Tea parties are trendy again, as people rediscover the simple pleasure of sharing with friends delicious morsels of food and piping hot tea. It is easy to prepare your own tea party: Just dust off your favorite tea set, polish your silverware, and follow these recipes!

Make sure you have plenty of tea on hand. You might want to brew pots of traditional favorites, such as Earl Grey and English Breakfast, as well as something lighter and more flowery, such as a jasmine or chamomile infusion. Serve teas with milk, sugar cubes, candy sticks, or tea straws.

As for the menu, almost anything goes. You can make traditional English favorites like crumpets and scones (see recipes, pages 23 and 25), or try a combination of favorites from Japan, China, and Russia. People often prepare miniature dishes for serving at teatime, arranging them elegantly on platters and serving on small plates. All of the recipes in the following chapter are bite-size or a bit bigger, making them suitable to be served in this way.

CREAM CHEESE TARTLETS

Show off the season's freshest fruit with these lovely tartlets (see photo, page 125).

INGREDIENTS

Makes 8 tartlets

Crust:

6 tablespoons unsalted butter, melted

1¼ cups crushed graham crackers

2 tablespoons sugar

Filling:

1 cup cream cheese

3½ ounces white chocolate, melted and cooled

¼ cup sour cream

1½ cups sliced fruit or berries

PREPARATION

1. Prepare the crust: In a small bowl, combine butter, graham crackers, and sugar. Distribute mixture evenly among eight 4-inch fluted tartlet pans with removable bottoms. Press along the bottom and up the sides of each pan to form a crust. Place pans on a baking sheet, cover with plastic wrap, and refrigerate until filling is prepared.

2. Prepare the filling: In a medium bowl, beat cream cheese with an electric mixer, until light and fluffy. Add melted chocolate and sour cream and beat until smooth.

3. Divide filling evenly between tartlet shells and smooth with a spatula. Cover with plastic wrap and refrigerate at least 1 hour, until firm. To serve, top each tartlet with fruit slices or whole berries.

MINI HEART PIZZAS

Pizza-lovers will be delighted to see these cheesy snacks at teatime!

INGREDIENTS

Makes 10 mini pizzas

Pizza crust:

2 teaspoons active dry yeast

1 teaspoon sugar

¾ cup warm water

2 cups all-purpose flour, plus more for dusting

½ teaspoon salt

Sauce:

8 tablespoons tomato paste

1 teaspoon olive oil

2 tablespoons brown sugar

1 clove garlic, crushed

1 teaspoon freshly squeezed lemon juice

1 handful fresh basil leaves, thinly sliced

Salt and freshly ground black pepper

Topping:

2 cups grated mozzarella cheese

1 tablespoon chopped fresh oregano

1 cup broccoli florets, blanched

1 small onion, finely chopped

½ small green pepper, finely diced

½ small red pepper, finely diced

½ small yellow pepper, finely diced

1 scallion, finely chopped

8 fresh button mushrooms, finely sliced

1 baby zucchini, thinly sliced

(continued on page 122)

(continued from page 121)

1 small eggplant, finely diced

1 small carrot, peeled and thinly sliced

2 tablespoons olive oil

1 tablespoon balsamic vinegar

1 teaspoon brown sugar

1 tablespoon dried sage

Salt and freshly ground black pepper

PREPARATION

1. Prepare the dough: In a small bowl, stir together yeast, sugar, and water until yeast is foamy and sugar dissolved.

2. In a separate bowl, sift together flour and salt. Add yeast mixture and stir until a firm dough forms. Turn dough out onto a lightly floured surface and knead until smooth and elastic. Cover with a dishcloth and let rise directly on counter 20 to 30 minutes, until doubled in size.

3. Prepare the sauce: In a heavy saucepan over medium heat, cook tomato paste, olive oil, brown sugar, garlic, lemon juice, basil, and salt and pepper to taste, stirring occasionally, about 10 to 15 minutes, until thick.

4. Prepare the topping: Preheat oven to 325°F. In a small bowl, combine cheese and oregano and set aside. Cut broccoli into bite-size pieces and transfer to a large bowl. Add onion, peppers, scallion, mushrooms, zucchini, eggplant, carrot, olive oil, balsamic vinegar, brown sugar, sage, and salt and pepper to taste, and toss to coat. Spread on a baking sheet and bake about 20 minutes, until tender. Transfer to a large bowl using a slotted spoon.

5. Assemble the pizzas: Line a baking sheet with parchment paper. On floured surface, roll out risen dough to ½ inch thick. Cut out individual pizzas using a large heart-shaped cookie cutter. Arrange on prepared baking sheet. Brush each heart with tomato paste and top with vegetables and cheese. Bake about 20 minutes, until bottom of crusts is brown and cheese is melted and golden. Serve warm.

WHITE CHOCOLATE MINI CAKES

Tangy lemon provides a lovely pause in the sweetness of the chocolate, and makes for a deliciously surprising combination.

INGREDIENTS

Makes 12 mini cakes

Cake:

1 cup butter, plus more for greasing

2 teaspoons grated lemon zest

2 teaspoons grated lime zest

6 ounces white chocolate, coarsely chopped

1½ cups superfine (castor) sugar

¾ cup whole milk

1½ cups all-purpose flour

½ cup self-rising flour

2 large free-range eggs, lightly beaten

Frosting:

7 ounces white chocolate, coarsely chopped

1½ cups confectioners' sugar

½ cup heavy cream

1 teaspoon freshly squeezed lemon juice

1 teaspoon grated lemon zest

PREPARATION

1. Preheat oven to 325°F and grease a 12-cup heart-shaped muffin pan with butter.

2. Prepare the cakes: In a medium saucepan over low heat, stir together butter, zests, chocolate, sugar, and milk until smooth. Transfer to a large heatproof bowl and let cool 15 to 20 minutes.

3. Sift together flours and stir into chocolate mixture. Mix in eggs. Pour batter into prepared muffin pan and bake about 50 to 60 minutes, until a toothpick inserted in the middle cupcake comes out clean. Let cool in pan 15 minutes, then turn out onto a wire rack, flip right side up, and let cool completely.

4. Prepare the frosting: Melt chocolate in the top of a double boiler. Gradually add sugar and cream, whisking until smooth. Remove from heat and stir in lemon juice and zest. If frosting is too thin, add a little more confectioners' sugar. Spread frosting on cakes and serve.

White Chocolate Mini Cakes (front) and Cream Cheese Tartlets (back)

FESTIVE CUPCAKES

These delicate cakes are reminiscent of fairytale childhood tea parties.

INGREDIENTS

Makes 24 cupcakes

Cupcakes:

½ cup butter, softened

½ teaspoon pure vanilla extract

¾ cup superfine (castor) sugar

3 large free-range eggs

2 cups self-rising flour

¼ cup whole milk

Frosting:

2 cups confectioners' sugar, sifted

1 tablespoon butter, melted

2 tablespoons hot water

¼ teaspoon pure vanilla extract

2 drops red food coloring

¼ teaspoon peppermint extract

1 teaspoon cocoa powder

1 tablespoon passion fruit pulp

Tiny candies for garnish

PREPARATION

1. Preheat oven to 350°F. Line two 12-cup muffin pans with paper liners.

2. Prepare the cupcakes: In a large bowl, beat together butter, vanilla, sugar, and eggs until smooth. Slowly mix in flour and milk, then beat for about 5 minutes, until mixture is smooth and pale in color.

3. Drop a heaping tablespoon of batter into each muffin cup. Bake about 20 minutes, until golden. Let cool 5 minutes in pan, then turn out onto a wire rack, flip right side up, and let cool completely.

4. Prepare the frosting: In a small bowl, mix together sugar and butter. Gradually add hot water, stirring with a fork to make a smooth paste.

5. Divide evenly between four small bowls. In each bowl, stir in one of the flavorings: vanilla and red food coloring (together), peppermint, cocoa, and passion fruit pulp.

6. Spread frosting evenly on cupcakes and decorate with candies.

INDEX

almonds
  Chinese Almond Cookies, 33
banana
  Walnut, Date, and Coconut Banana Loaf, 55
Blini, 66
Buttermilk Scones, 26
cakes
  Festive Cupcakes, 126
  Pecan Tea Cakes, 62
  Plum Cake, 64
  Spiced Honey Cake, 63
  White Chocolate Mini Cakes, 124
chai
  Chai Latte, 90
  Chocolate Chai, 85
  Kashmiri Chai, 86
  Very Spicy Chai, 85
chamomile
  Chamomile-Infused White Chocolate Sauce, 110
  Creamy Potato Chamomile Soup, 108
  Iced Chamomile, Lemon, and Lavender Tea, 78
  tisane, 96
cheese
  Cheddar Cheese and Chive Scones, 26
  Cheddar Cheese with Chutney Butter, 22
  Cream Cheese Tartlets, 121
  Goat Cheese and Watercress, 20
  Japanese-Style Cheesecake, 47
  Mini Heart Pizzas, 121
  Smoked Salmon with Ginger Butter, 19
chicken
  Tea-Smoked Chicken, 103
chocolate
  Chamomile-Infused White Chocolate Sauce, 110
  Chocolate Chai, 85
  Chocolate-Covered Strawberries, 64
  Double Chocolate Scones, 26

White Chocolate Mini Cakes, 124
chutney
  Green Mango Chutney, 55
cider
  Hot Cider Tea, 88
citrus
  Citrus Blend tisane, 95
  Citrus Scones, 26
  Jasmine and Citrus Pound Cake, 114
Classic Iced Tea, 71
coconut
  Coconut Ladoos, 56
  Coconut Rice Squares, 42
  Walnut, Date, and Coconut Banana Loaf, 55
cookies
  Cardamom Butter Cookies, 54
  Chinese Almond Cookies, 33
  Festive Fortune Cookies, 34
  Walnut Ginger Cookies, 66
corn
  Curried Corn Patties, 53
cranberry
  Cranberry Iced Tea Cooler, 75
  Spicy Cranberry Tea, 90
crumpets
  Traditional Crumpets, 23
curd
  Lemon Curd, 24
dates
  Walnut, Date, and Coconut Banana Loaf, 55
Dorayaki, 46
egg
  Egg Salad Flowers, 22
  Marbled Tea Eggs, 110
Elderflower tisane, 96
Fennel tisane, 96
ginger
  Ginger and Honey Tea Cubes, 80
  Iced Honey, Lime, and Ginger Tea, 75
  Smoked Salmon with Ginger Butter, 19

tisane, 98
  Walnut Ginger Cookies, 66
green tea
  Green Tea Ice Cream, 116
  Green Tea Loaf, 44
Honey Butter, 25
Iced Apple and Spice Tea, 76
Iced Honey, Lime, and Ginger Tea, 75
Iced Spice Tea, 72
jasmine
  Iced Jasmine Tea, 72
  Jasmine and Citrus Pound Cake, 114
lavender
  Iced Chamomile, Lemon, and Lavender Tea, 78
  Lavender Shortbread Cookies, 112
  Lavender Whipped Cream, 116
Linden Flowers tisane, 95
mango
  Green Mango Chutney, 55
  Mango Muffins, 36
Milky Vanilla Tea, 88
Mint Tea Punch, 74
Pecan Tea Cakes, 62
peppermint
  Peppermint Lamb Chops, 106
  tisane, 98
  White Fish in Peppermint and Lemon Tea, 106
pizza
  Mini Heart Pizzas, 121
Plum Cake, 64
rice
  Coconut Rice Squares, 42
  Creamy Rice Pudding, 54
Rooibos
  Rooibos Couscous with Snow Peas and Shitake Mushrooms, 104
  tisane, 98
salmon
  Smoked Salmon with Ginger Butter, 19

Tea-Smoked Salmon, 103
sandwiches
  Cheddar Cheese with Chutney Butter, 22
  Cucumber and Mint, 20
  Egg Salad Flowers, 22
  Goat Cheese and Watercress, 20
  Smoked Salmon with Ginger Butter, 19
scones
  Buttermilk Scones, 26
  Cheddar Cheese and Chive Scones, 26
  Citrus Scones, 26
  Double Chocolate Scones, 26
  Dried Fruit Scones, 26
  Spiced Scones, 26
  Traditional Scones, 25
  Whole-Wheat Raisin Scones, 26
semolina
  Rava Ladoos, 56
sencha
  Iced Sencha Tea, 76
shortbread
  Scottish Shortbread, 24
strawberries
  Chocolate-Covered Strawberries, 64
Sun Tea, 74
Sweet Southern Iced Tea, 71
syrup, sugar, 71
tea
  about, 6-13
tea cubes
  Ginger and Honey Tea Cubes, 80
  Lemon Lime Tea Cubes, 80
Tea Nog, 86
Thai Iced Tea, 78
walnuts
  Candied Walnuts, 33
  Walnut Scones, 26
  Walnut, Date, and Coconut Banana Loaf, 55

128